Teaching from the Tabernacle

Teaching from the Tabernacle

Roy Lee DeWitt

BAKER BOOK HOUSE
Grand Rapids, Michigan 49516

Copyright 1986 by Roy L. DeWitt

First reprinted 1988 by Baker Book House Company
with permission of the copyright owner

Library of Congress Catalog Card Number: 86-60046

ISBN: 0-8010-2987-2

Fifth printing, September 1993

Scripture quotations are taken from the King James Version

Drawings by Wayne Boostrom
Photographs by Dean Lanckton

Printed in the United States of America

To my Family:
Suk Cha, Sylas, Lydia, and **Titus DeWitt**

The publication of this book is the culmination of efforts by many individuals.

I want to thank my wife, Suk Cha, for her understanding, patience and spiritual support during the construction of my scale model of the tabernacle and the research and the writing of the manuscript. Her skill as a seamstress on the high priest garments and the appropriate parts of the tabernacle is greatly appreciated.

Many thanks to Wayne Boostrom for his careful illustrations.

I am grateful for the financial and prayer support of my ministry over the years by Larry and Tony Deraps. Their friendship and encouragement has sustained me.

I want to especially thank my brother, Lee DeWitt, Jr. I can say without reservation that this book is as much a product of his labor as my own. My lack of writing experience required that he wrestle with my original manuscript more than should be required of any editor.

A selection of 50 slides, may be obtained by writing:

Roy Lee DeWitt
993 Camellia Drive
Marietta, GA 30062

Contents

Charles   9
List of Photographs   11
Names of the Tabernacle   13
Preface   15

Part One
Background Information

1. The Importance of the Tabernacle   19
2. The History of the Tabernacle   25
3. The Material and Construction of the Tabernacle   41
   Material   43
       Metals • Fabrics • Skins • Wood • Oil and Spices • Stones
   Defining the Three Areas of the Tabernacle   49
   Court of the Tabernacle   50
       Door of the Tabernacle • Altar • Laver
   The Tabernacle Proper   56
       The Four-Layer Covering • Walls • Pillars and Veils • Candlestick
       • Table of Shewbread • Altar of Incense • Ark and Mercy Seat
4. The Levitical Priesthood   73
   Their Call   75
   Their Consecration   79
       Presentation • Washing • Clothing • Anointing • Offerings
5. The Typology of the Tabernacle   99

Part Two
Panoramic View of the Tabernacle

6. The Court of the Tabernacle and Its Offerings and Furnishings   117
   The Brazen Altar   118
   The Five Principal Offerings   120
       The Animal Parts of the Offerings • The Significance of the
       Offerings • The Sin Offering • The Trespass Offering • The Burnt
       Offering • The Meat Offering • The Peace Offering

7

The Ritual of the Sin Offering   150
Tithes, First Fruits and Firstborn   153
Drink Offering   154
Laver   154
7. The Holy Place and Its Furnishings   161
    Candlestick   162
    Table of Shewbread   165
    Altar of Incense   167
    The Ritual of the Daily Burnt Offering   170
8. The Holy of Holies and the Ark   177
    The Ritual of the Day of Atonement   182
    Bibliography   191
    Index   193

Charts and Illustrations

Estimated number of people in the exodus   28
Exodus route   34
Chronological chart of nation of Israel and the construction of the tabernacle   35
Map of the tabernacle and ark in the promised land   38
Chronological chart of tabernacle locations after entry into Canaan   39
Estimated present day cost to build the tabernacle   50
Bezaleel makes the ark   69
Stones of the breastplate   70
Areas of the tabernacle   71
Tabernacle roof   72
Moses anoints Aaron with oil   85
Levites erect the tabernacle   89
Four generations   95
High priest   96
Placement of the tabernacle   97
Coverings for the furniture   98
Types of antitypes   103
An Israelite brings his offering to the tabernacle   122
A priest inspects a sacrificial offering   124
Sin offering   135
Trespass offering   139
Burnt offering   141
Meat offering   145
Peace offering   149
Compulsory offerings for the nation of Israel   155

List of Photographs

The tabernacle   19
Worshiper at the tabernacle   25
The tabernacle under construction   41
Urim and thummim   49
Court of the tabernacle   51
Linen curtain   52
Door of the tabernacle   53
Altar   54
Grate of the altar   55
Laver   56
Tabernacle proper   57
Badger skin covering   60
Ram skin covering   60
Goat hair covering   60
Fine linen covering   60
Walls of the tabernacle   61
Walls showing the bars   62
Pillars and veils   63
Second set of pillars and second veil   64
Candlestick   65
Table of shewbread   66
Altar of incense   67
Ark and mercy seat with contents   68
The high priest   73
Shoulderpieces   82
Breastplate   83
Ephod with pomegranate ornaments and bells   83
Mitre with gold plate   84
Shadows of heavenly things   99
The court of the tabernacle and its furnishings   117
The ritual of the sin offering   151
The holy place and its furnishings   161
The ritual of the daily burnt offering   173
The high priest at the ark in the holy of holies   177
The ritual of the day of atonement   184

Names of the Tabernacle

The Tabernacle of the Congregation (Exod. 27:21)
The Tabernacle of Testimony (Exod. 38:21)
The Tabernacle of the Tent of the Congregation (Exod. 39:32)
The Tabernacle of the Lord (Lev. 17:4)
The Tabernacle of the Witness (Num. 17:7)
The Lord's Tabernacle (Josh. 22:19)
Temple of the Lord (1 Sam. 1:9)
The Tabernacle of the House of God (1 Chron. 6:48)

Preface

This book was conceived in response to the need for a concise and simple presentation of how to properly identify and understand the types found in the tabernacle. In treating the subject, I felt it best to set it within the framework of a general study of the tabernacle.

Therefore the first five chapters, which make up Part One, deal with background information, of which every student should be familiar when he studies the tabernacle. Chapter 1 explains why an understanding of the tabernacle is important to Christians. Chapter 2 traces the history of the tabernacle. Chapter 3 describes the materials and construction of the tabernacle. Chapter 4 discusses the Levitical priesthood. Chapter 5 discusses the important subject of typology. Here I explain how to define a type and present guidelines for the interpretation and explanation of biblical types.

The last three chapters, Part Two, treat typically each of the three areas of the tabernacle and their furnishings: the outer court, the holy place and the holy of holies. Together these chapters provide a panoramic view of the tabernacle as a type.

In addition, I have included maps, photographs of my scale model of the tabernacle and original charts and information sheets.

Although I have made application of the principles for interpretation of the types found in the tabernacle, I have deliberately avoided burdening the reader with lengthy examples. Instead, my objective was to gather the factual information necessary for a proper interpretation. This will enable others to apply these truths accurately.

Roy L. DeWitt
Chatham, Illinois 1986

PART 1

Background Information

These five chapters lay a foundation for a meaningful in-depth study of the tabernacle. Often the material treated here is not taken into consideration or given its proper place in a serious study of the tabernacle.

The Importance of the Tabernacle

Neither by the blood of goats and calves, but by his own blood he entered in once into the holy place, having obtained eternal redemption for us (Heb. 9:12).

The tabernacle

Generally speaking, Christians today do not recognize the underlying principles of salvation to the Old Testament saints and first-century Christians (Heb. 8:2, 9:9–11). Overlooking the valuable lessons of the tabernacle, one misses a great opportunity to fully understand and appreciate the redemptive work of Jesus Christ. One must understand that the principles of salvation have never changed. God's plan of salvation was established at the foundation of the world and its principles have been observed by every child of God since, whether it was Abel offering his "excellent sacrifice" at the beginning of history, the Israelites offering their sacrifices at the tabernacle in the wilderness or you accepting by faith the propitiatory work of Jesus.

The tabernacle performed a particularly special role in revealing God's principles and plan of salvation, especially to the Jews. Too often we forget that Christianity has its roots in Judaism. Jesus was a Jew, and all but one of the writers of the New Testament was a Jew. This makes it all the more important that one understands the relationship between Judaism (the tabernacle sacrifices) and Christianity (the sacrifice of Jesus). The laws and history given in the Pentateuch are the platform on which the rest of the Bible stands. Misunderstanding in this area can lead to false teachings about God's character and his plan of salvation.

Although the difference between worshiping God at the tabernacle under the Old Testament Covenant and worshiping him under the New Covenant is profound, the principles are identical. How else can one understand the Bible when it speaks of Christ's death as from the foundation of the world (Rev. 13:8)? Also, in Romans 3:25, 26, we see the efficacy of Christ's death for Old Testament saints as well. The same is expressed in Hebrews 9:15. For this reason, I believe the salvation experiences of the Old Testament saints were identical to ours today! Who can say they didn't experience, at least inwardly, the same shameful awareness of their sinfulness, the same contrite heart, and a repugnance at what is unholy and a dependence on God's sacrifice for the atonement of their sins? Keeping this in mind, one can see there need not be any difference. Only the revealed stage of the plan of redemption has changed (Heb. 9:10).

Although God has used various means to express his plan of redemption, the requirement for man to appropriate it hasn't changed. It has always been by faith in the propitiation of Christ. The tangibleness of the Mosaic economy with its observance of rituals at the tabernacle never saved a soul. It served only to portray the reality of God's reconciliation to his people and therefore served as a tangible way in which they could express their faith in the sacrifice God provided. Though the ceremonial aspects made their expression of faith more physical, it did not lessen the relationship they could have with God, for if the heart was not right and there was not a recognition of the divine intention, it availed them nothing.

Thus, worship at the tabernacle was central to the spiritual well-being of the Israelites, and only when we begin to understand that God dealt with them as he does with us, will we begin to see the tremendous importance of the tabernacle.

Perhaps another reason few Christians see the importance of the tabernacle has to do with the general belief that it was used for only forty years when, in fact, it was used for 647 years (see page 35). In addition, when the tabernacle was no longer in use, Israel came to Jerusalem to worship God at Solomon's temple, which continued the same means of approaching God. Therefore, the nation of Israel, from its birth to the death of Christ, a period of 1,700 years, approached God with the same system initiated originally with the tabernacle in the wilderness. The fact that the Israelites used the tabernacle and its system of worship for hundreds of years should certainly indicate it importance. Present-day Christians may still glean something from a study of the tabernacle, as the writer of Hebrews so wonderfully reveals.

Another factor that emphasized the tabernacle's importance was its location at the center of the camp and the position of the Levites, who camped nearby to guard against unlawful approach. The other tribes also camped around the tabernacle but at a distance. The tabernacle was also at the center of the nation during marches (Num. 10:17).

Joshua followed this same principle in the Promised Land when he established the tabernacle at Shiloh, a city in the geographical center of the nation, even though the tribes were separated after the dividing up of the land. At this time, the tribes were scattered some distance from the tabernacle, and later, the temple. We see God's foresight in commanding that sacrifices be made only at the tabernacle (Lev. 17:1–9) and that all males assemble there before the Lord three times a year. These laws were instituted to assure that the Israelites continued to use the proper means of approaching God.

The events surrounding the giving of the pattern for the tabernacle also point to its importance. The pattern was given to Moses on his sixth ascent of Mount Sinai when God gave the law. Therefore, with the giving of a greater revelation of God's law, there was also a giving of a greater revelation of God's reconciliation with his people. This is a tremendously important fact that is often overlooked. It was also an important occasion for mankind; for God, in giving his moral standards to the Israelites, also gave them to the world. "What nation is there so great, that hath statutes and judgments so righteous as all this law?" (Deut. 4:8). These laws, which pertained to every aspect of their lives, guided them in their infancy as a nation and set them apart as a peculiar nation, even to this day. It has taken other nations, apart from the biblical revelation, many hundreds of years to understand the need of laws similar to those God gave the Israelites.

The Bible records how great these laws are, but, just as importantly, it reveals the result of neglecting them—divine punishment. The seesaw relationship Israel had with God was always as a result of their obedience or disobedience to these laws (Heb. 3:8–19). God's justice demands punishment for disobedience. When penalty is not inflicted, it encourages rebellion. However, God desired to extend mercy to the Israelites. This had to be undertaken wisely. As good as laws are, once broken, they can only bring condemnation and demand the infliction of a penalty. Paul said, "If there had been a law given which could have given life, verily righteousness should have been by the law" (Gal. 3:21). The principle involved here is that once a law is broken it can never justify, only demand that its penalty be inflicted upon the law breaker. This does not make the law bad at all. What law can justify once it is broken? The problem that confronted God was how he could extend mercy to the Israelites and, at the same time, uphold his law. To do this without consideration for his law would encourage rebellion.

Thus, we see the great importance of the tabernacle; it would be through the tabernacle that God would demonstrate, in "shadow," how he would extend his mercy without abolishing his law. Through the tabernacle, the Israelites had the gospel preached to them: "For unto us was the gospel preached, as well as unto them" (Heb. 4:2). This is the most important lesson of the tabernacle, and one that should continually be kept in mind. Failure to see this central theme has possibly led to more confusion about the tabernacle and God's character than any other misunderstanding of God's Word. The gospel preached to them by object lesson—through the tabernacle, its priesthood, rituals, offerings and furniture—was based upon the same principles found in the New Testament Gospel.

If the tabernacle is to be a true type of the gospel then the similarity between them must be real! God didn't have two gospels; rather, when Christ came he revealed the Gospel that was concealed in the "shadow" of the tabernacle. This in no way moderated the salvation of the Israelites, for they were never justified by the law; rather, they were justified by faith as we are presently. The only thing lacking in the Gospel preached through the tabernacle was that Christ had not yet died as the Lamb slain from the foundation of the world.

The History of the Tabernacle

"Let my people go, that they may serve me" (Exod. 9:1).

Worshiper at the tabernacle

Because the record of events surrounding the tabernacle's origin, use, and travel is inexorably linked to the history of Israel, a historical study of the tabernacle is more than a study of the tabernacle alone. It is also a study of the nation of Israel.

Israel, as an independent nation, and the tabernacle came into existence at about the same time for a mutual reason; consequently, they shared the divine purpose of revealing a significant part of God's unfolding revelation of himself to mankind.

Israel was chosen to be the nation through which the world would be divinely blessed, and the tabernacle was chosen to represent how this blessing would be accomplished. The first prophetic mention concerning the sojourn of the nation of Israel and the materials for the construction of the tabernacle is found in Genesis 15:13–14. To fully appreciate the tabernacle we need to study the birth of Israel and the impact the tabernacle had on the nation. In addition, a study of the tabernacle's history will help one to appreciate its role in preparing the world for the arrival of Christ, of which the tabernacle is the "shadow" and the nation of Israel is a "vehicle."

Use of the chart at the end of this chapter will help the reader to better understand the historical setting of the tabernacle. The chart begins with the first scriptural mention of the nation of Israel and continues to the dedication of Solomon's temple, when the tabernacle was brought to Jerusalem. It will help the reader to understand this period of history as well as grasp the chronological sequence of events associated with the tabernacle. The reader should refer to it frequently. Note that the chart graphically illustrates that the tabernacle was used much longer than the forty years generally accepted.

The chart is also valuable in solving some seemingly contradictory facts. For instance, the first glimpse of the nation of Israel is found in Genesis 12 and 15. In Genesis 12:1–3, God promised Abram that from his seed would come a nation that would bless all the families of the earth and in Genesis 15:13 that this nation would be afflicted for 400 years. Yet, at the time of the Exodus (Exod. 12:40–41), when the affliction ceased, this period is said to be 430 years long. This same period is said to be 400 years in Acts 7:6 and again 430 years in Galatians 3:16–18.

Can both periods be right? An investigation of scripture provides an explanation. The 430-year period began with Abram's call (Gen. 12:1–4) and the 400-year period began with the confirmation of Isaac as the seed (Gen. 22:15–18), which began thirty years after the call of Abram. Abram was called when he was seventy-five years old and Isaac was born twenty-five years later (Gen. 21:5). This gives twenty-five of the thirty years difference, so Isaac must have been five years old when he was confirmed as that seed.

The 430-year period is found by adding the following periods of history: from the call of Abraham to the birth of Isaac (Gen. 12:4), twenty-five years; from the birth of Isaac to Jacob's birth

The History of the Tabernacle

(Gen. 25:26), sixty years; from Jacob's birth to his death (Gen. 47:28), 147 years; from the death of Jacob to the death of Joseph (Gen. 41:46, 53; 45:6, 11; 47:9, 28; 50:22), fifty-four years; and from Joseph's death to the Exodus, which is found by subtracting the total years thus far, or 286, from the 430-year total, which leaves 144 years.

With this information, it is possible to determine how long the Israelites were actually in Egypt. Since the sojourn in Egypt began when Jacob came there with his family, we have only to add the period beginning with his arrival in Egypt, which is seventeen years of his 147-year lifespan (Gen. 47:9 or 47:28), to the fifty-four years from the death of Jacob to the death of Joseph and the 144 years from Joseph's death to the Exodus. These figures give a total of 215 years in which the Israelites remained in Egypt, half of the 430 years that they sojourned.

This information can also help in understanding the reference to the fourth generation found in Genesis 15:16 (See chart on page 95). Its phrase, "they shall come hither again," implies that they must leave and return to Canaan. When did they leave? When Jacob came to Egypt. When did they return? When Moses led them back to the Promised Land 215 years later, which is exactly four generations: Jacob to Levi, Levi to Kohath, Kohath to Amram and Amram to Moses (Gen. 35:23; Exod. 6:16, 18, 20).

The greatest event of Israeli history, their Exodus from Egypt after 215 years of Egyptian servitude, began when God heard their cries (Exod. 2:24; 3:7) and sent Moses to lead them back to the Promised Land. While they were in Egypt, the Israelites had increased from a mere seventy individuals (Exod. 1:5) to more than three million. We find in Exodus 12:37, 38 that their first census was taken as they departed Egypt. The following figures provide an estimate of how many Israelites departed from Egypt.

Although Israel was large enough to constitute a small nation, it was actually no more than a large group of liberated slaves who were unacquainted with war, self-government or God. This is the reason God chose not to take them to the Promised Land by a direct route (Exod. 13:17, 18). Instead, they traveled by way of the wilderness of the Red Sea to Mount Sinai, where God began to establish them as a nation (see map, page 38).

From Egypt, the Israelites sojourned forty-five days before reaching Mount Sinai. While they were in the wilderness, God

Table 1 **Estimated Number of People in the Exodus**

Men of war (Exod. 12:37, Num. 1:3)	600,000
Wives of the men of war	600,000
Children of the men of war (3 to a family)	1,800,000
Levites:	
Males one month and older (Num. 3:39)	22,300
30–50 year old wives of Levites (Num. 4:47, 48)	8,580
Children of the Levites (3 to a family)	25,740
Those not counted:	
Men too old to go to war	
Men too young to go to war	
Wives and children of the above	
All females of the tribe of Levites not married to a male between the ages of 30 and 50	
Mixed multitudes that came out of Egypt with the Israelites (Gen. 45:10; Num. 11:4; Exod. 12:38)	
Total	3,056,620

(Those not counted could significantly increase the total.)

gave them the laws necessary to govern themselves. Christians should never underestimate the importance of those laws to the Israelites and the influence they have had on the rest of the world. The civil and moral laws they received have become the basis for the laws of all nations where one finds enlightened men (Deut. 4:5–8). During the first three months, Moses ascended Mount Sinai eight times to receive these laws from God. Two of those ascensions lasted forty days. The sixth ascension, the first of the forty-day meetings, is important to this study because it was when God gave Moses the pattern for the tabernacle.

It may have been the will of God for Moses to begin construction of the tabernacle when he descended this time, but instead, Moses faced a crisis situation upon his descent to the camp. The Israelites, who had earlier heard God deliver the decalogue and had agreed to keep it, nevertheless had quickly turned to idolatry. It was only Moses' intercession that prevented God from consuming Israel in his wrath (Exod. 32:10–11).

Therefore, the construction of the tabernacle did not begin for another forty-two days, or four months and eleven days after the Israelites' departure from Egypt. During the next seven months (the length of time it took to construct the tabernacle), anointed workers constructed it from the freewill (heave) offerings of the congregation, according to the pattern Moses received from the Lord on Mount Sinai. Eleven months and fifteen days after their departure from Egypt, the tabernacle was completed and set up

(Exod. 40:17), but only after the approval of Moses that all had been done as the Lord had commanded (Exod. 39:43). (There is another tabernacle mentioned in Exodus 33:7–11, which was constructed on a temporary basis and should not be confused with the tabernacle of the wilderness.)

It was at this time that the pillar of cloud, which had guided them from Egypt, covered the tabernacle and the glory of the Lord filled it. The presence of the cloud over the tabernacle signified the guiding presence of the Lord. When it rested over the tabernacle, they were to rest, and when it was taken up, they were to follow.

Fifty days later, the pillar of cloud was taken up for the first time (Num. 10:11), and the Israelites began their journey to the Promised Land. They had been at Mount Sinai for eleven months and twenty days. While they were there, God had revealed to them everything necessary for their well-being; their well-being was dependent on their obedience.

In Deuteronomy 1:2 we find that their move from Horeb (Mount Sinai) to Kadesh-barnea, located in the southern part of the Promised Land, was an eleven-day journey. Yet it took them almost forty years to complete the trip to the Promised Land. Why? In the fifteen chapters that deal with this period of history (Num. 11–26) we witness complaints, lust of the flesh, the rebellion of Miriam and Aaron against Moses, the nation's rebellion at Kadesh-barnea, the rebellion of Korah in seeking the priesthood, and Israel's sin through the teaching of Balaam. For thirty-eight years of that forty-year period, there is complete silence since the events covered in the fifteen chapters deal only with the first and last year of the forty years of wandering.

The forty years were literally years of waste, a revealing testimony of the effects of disobedience. The second numbering of the nation reflects this. After almost forty years the Israeli population of men able to go to war decreased by 1,820, silent proof of how complaining and disobedience hold back the programs of God.

In Numbers 33:19–49 we find a summary of their journey during the wilderness wanderings. These verses locate the various encampments after their departure from Mount Sinai and on their way to Shittim, which is on the plain of Moab bordering the Promised Land. Apparently, these were the more permanent camps. This can be substantiated by the fact that from their journey from Mount Sinai to Kadesh (Rithmah) only two camps are mentioned (Num. 33:16–18). Being an eleven-day journey (Deut. 1:2), it is certain they had to camp many times, probably each evening.

The encampments listed in Numbers 33 are probably those where they camped for an entire day or more (Num. 9:22).

When they entered the Promised Land they camped at Gigal (Josh. 4:19)(see map page 35), which is between the Jordan River and Jericho. Although it is not stated, there is little doubt that the tabernacle was set up here for the five years it took for them to conquer the land from the Canaanites. At the end of the five years, the whole congregation assembled at Shiloh. It was there that the seven tribes, which had not yet received their inheritance, had the land divided to them by lots. Here the tabernacle was set up (Josh. 18:1) and used for 470 years.

Although the arrival of the tabernacle in Shiloh marked the beginning of a bright future, its departure from Shiloh heralded a dark period in Israeli history. In 1 Samuel 4 we see the Israelites defeated by the Philistines who captured the ark. Also, Shiloh and possibly the tabernacle were destroyed by them at this time (Ps. 78:60–61; Jer. 7:12; 26:6). It was at this time that God determined to make his permanent dwelling in Jerusalem (Ps. 78:67–68). With the permanent separation of the ark and the tabernacle, it becomes necessary to follow their histories separately.

There is no scriptural mention of the tabernacle for the next seventy years. This may indicate its destruction, but not in the sense that it was total, which would contradict 1 Chronicles 21:29 and 2 Chronicles 1:5. That the material parts, curtains, and veils were burnt, and the walls, pillars, and furniture uprooted, as depicted in 1 Chronicles 17:5, is a reasonable interpretation.

The next mention of the tabernacle is at Nob (1 Sam. 21:1–9). When and why it was taken there is not clear. The incident of David eating the shewbread and his receiving the sword of Goliath occurred at Nob. Jesus refers to this in Mark 2:26 and Matthew 12:2–6. Saul, the King of Israel, on hearing that David had been at Nob, became jealous, destroyed the city, and killed eighty-five priests.

It is not known if the tabernacle was destroyed at this time, but, if so, it was rebuilt and transferred to Gibeon; for it is mentioned there about ten to fifteen years later during David's reign as king. We know it was already at Gibeon at that time (1 Chron. 16:39). The tabernacle had probably been set up after the death of Saul, but before the unity of the nation under King David. Very likely it was set up by the "house" of Saul during the early part of the seven-year division of the nation after Saul's death in an effort to unify the tribes that were following Saul's successors.

During this same period we need to keep in mind that David built a tabernacle in Jerusalem to house the ark, which is the only holy vessel ever mentioned in use at the tabernacle of David. Apparently, the other vessels remained with the Mosaic tabernacle at Gibeon (1 Sam. 21:6, 1 Chron. 21:29 and 2 Chron. 1:3–5). This distinction is necessary to prevent confusion about the two tabernacles. Even with the separation of the ark from the tabernacle, the nation continued to go to Gibeon to make their animal sacrifices (1 Chron. 16:37–40). The two tabernacles explain why there were two High Priests during David's reign (2 Sam. 8:17).

The original (Mosaic) tabernacle was moved from Gibeon to Jerusalem when Solomon dedicated the temple there. That this is the original tabernacle of Moses is proved by 1 Kings 8:4 and 2 Chronicles 5:5, which state that, along with the original tabernacle, all the holy vessels were brought. The only part of the original tabernacle that was incorporated into the temple was the ark, so the original tabernacle, along with its furniture, was probably put into storage. From here its history ends in obscurity.

The length of time the Mosaic tabernacle was used can be deduced by adding the following periods of history. The first period is from the time the tabernacle was originally set up until the crossing of the Jordan River, which was forty years. The next period covers from the crossing of the Jordan River until the events of the Book of Joshua end. We know from Joshua 14:7, 10 that there were five years of conquest, but how much time is covered after this is not known. Josephus, a first-century historian, states that Joshua was eighty-five years old when he took over for Moses. If this is true, then the duration of this period would be about twenty-five years, considering Joseph died when he was 110 (Josh. 24:29). The next period covers from the reign of the judges to the reign of Samuel and was 450 years (Acts 13:20). Samuel's reign is generally believed to be forty years. The reign of King Saul (Acts 13:21) and the reign of King David (2 Sam. 5:4) were each forty years. From the beginning of Solomon's reign to the dedication of the temple, when the tabernacle was brought there to be stored, twelve years passed. The temple was completed the eleventh year of Solomon's reign and was dedicated eleven months later (1 Kings 6:37–38), for a twelve-year total.

These figures (40, 25, 450, 40, 40, 40, and 12) establish that the tabernacle was used for 647 years, much longer than many people realize. At first glance, 1 Kings 6:1 seems to dispute the 647-year total. First Kings 6:1 covers the period from the Exodus to the fourth year of Solomon's reign. This period is stated as 480 years long. The disagreement can be reconciled if we understand that the 480-year period does not include some periods of Israelite history at this time.

This can be explained if one subtracts the 450 years that the Israelites were ruled by judges (Acts 13:20) from the 480-year span of 1 Kings 6:1, there are only thirty years left to include their wandering in the wilderness (forty years), the events of the Book of Joshua (twenty-five years), the judgeship of Samuel (forty years) and the reigns of Saul and David (forty years each). This is not possible. However, by adding to the 480 years those years they were not secure as a nation: the forty-year wandering, the five years of conquest, the 111 years of servitude, and the three years of civil strife found in Judges, a total of 639 years is apparent. The 647 years the tabernacle was used is figured to the twelfth year of Solomon's reign, so it is necessary to subtract eight years to arrive at the fourth year of his reign, because the 480-year period ended at the fourth year of Solomon's reign. This gives a 639-year total; thus the 480-year period also confirms that the tabernacle was used for 647 years.

To trace the history of the ark, we will begin with its capture by the Philistines. It was taken to Ashdod, then Gath, and finally to Ekron after its capture (1 Sam. 5). The Philistines experienced the judgment of God at each location; therefore, after seven months they decided to return the ark to the Israelites. The Philistines tested God's will and put the ark on a driverless cart drawn by two cows. Against odds, the cows took the ark directly to the Israeli town of Beth-shemesh, despite the baying of their calves (1 Sam. 6:1–12).

The Beth-shemites rejoiced to have the ark returned, but after experiencing the judgment of God when they looked into the ark, a prohibited act, they sought the men of nearby Kirjath-jearim to take it (1 Sam. 6:14–21).

Thus, for the next twenty years, the ark was at Kirjath-jearim in the house of Abinadab (1 Sam. 7:1–2). It is evident that those twenty years covered only the period up to Samuel's defeat of the Philistines (1 Sam. 7), because approximately eighty-seven years later David went to the house of Abinadab to recover the ark (1 Sam. 6:1–4 and 1 Chron. 13:5–7) and bring it to Jerusalem. Why he did not reunite the ark with the tabernacle, which was at Gibeon, is not known.

Nevertheless, the attempt to bring the ark to Jerusalem failed when Uzzah, the son of Abinadab, touched the ark and was killed by the Lord (2 Sam. 6:2–7 and 1 Chron. 13:6–10). David became afraid and left the ark with Obed-edom the Gittite (2 Sam 6:10). Gittites were the inhabitants of Gath, a city of Philistia, although some Gittites dwelt near Jerusalem (2 Sam. 15:18 and 19). It seems unlikely that David would have taken the ark to Obed-edom in Gath, some twenty-five miles away and in Philistine territory. Probably Obed-edom was a convert to Judaism and lived near Jerusalem with the other expatriates from Gath.

Three months later, David heard that the Lord had blessed Obed-edom (2 Sam. 6:11), so he went to him and brought the ark to Jerusalem where he placed it in the tabernacle he had constructed (1 Chron. 15:1, 16:1, 2 Chron. 5:5 and 2 Sam. 6:17), not the tabernacle Moses had constructed at Mount Sinai. This was during the seventh year of his reign (2 Sam. 5:4–5).

The unexpected death of Uzzah had caused David to search the scriptures, and he acknowledged that he had not sought the Lord properly (1 Chron. 15:13–15). Thus, on the second attempt to bring the ark to Jerusalem, the Levites were properly sanctified, and so they carried the ark on their shoulders according to the law of Moses (Exod. 25:14; Num. 4:5, 7:9; Deut. 31:9).

Then, about forty-five years later, the ark was placed in Solomon's temple at the time of its dedication (1 Kings 8:6–8 and 2 Chron. 5:7–9). When the ark was put in the Holy of Holies, the staves were partially removed from their rings (1 Kings 8:8 and 2 Chron. 5:9). This was meant to signify that the ark had found a permanent resting place and was not to be borne anymore (Exod. 25:15).

Although the ark did remain in the temple for a number of

years, this was not its final resting place. During the Babylonian captivity some 400 years later, the ark was probably taken from the temple during one of the three deportations. Although the ark is not mentioned specifically, there is reference to "all" of the vessels of the temple being taken to Babylon (2 Chron. 36:7, 10, 18).

The only additional reference to the ark is found in 2 Machabees 2:4–8, an apocryphal book that says the tabernacle, the ark, and the altar of incense were taken by Jeremiah and hidden in a cave on Mount Nebo. This is doubted by many Bible scholars, and seems to contradict Jeremiah 3:16. Neither the Book of Ezra nor the Book of Nehemiah, which refer to the return of the Israelites from the captivity, mention the ark (Ezra 1:7–11; 6:5). Thus, like the tabernacle, the history of the ark ends in obscurity.

The History of the Tabernacle

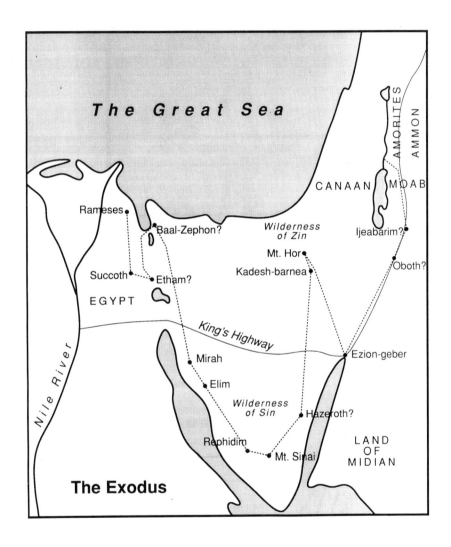

Chronological Chart of the Nation of Israel and the Construction of the Tabernacle

The call of Abram. Beginning 430 yrs. sojourning. Gen. 12:1–3

30th year Confirmation of Isaac as the seed. Beginning of the 400 yrs.

215th year End of Abram and his descendants sojourn in Canaan. Jacob goes to Egypt. Beginning of the sojourn in Egypt. Beginning of the four generations of Gen. 15:16. Gen 47:7–9

Time span from the Exodus

Time span from arrival at Mt. Sinai

First Month	Second Month	Third Month	Fourth Month	Fifth Month	Sixth Month	Seventh Month	Eighth M...
		46th day / 49th day	89th day		4th month, 11th day		
		4th day	44th day		86th day		

Day 1 Beginning of months for the nation of Israel. Exod. 12:2

Day 14 The Exodus End of the 430 yrs. of sojourning. Exod. 12:40–42; Num. 33:3

Day 1 Arrival at Mt. Sinai. Exod. 19:1

Day 14 Moses comes down from Mt. Sinai and finds people in idolatry. Levites chosen as ministers. Exod. 32

Day 26 Moses puts the law in an ark (not the ark of the tabernacle Deut 10:5). Material for the tabernacles construction brought daily. Exod. 36:3 Moses approves the construction of the tabernacle. Exod. 39:43

Day 2 Three days to sanctify the people. Exod. 19:10–11

Day 4 Moses writes the law. People agree to obey it. Exod. 24:4–8

Fifth ascent and descent of Mt. Sinai by Moses. Priest, 70 elders, have banquet with God. Exod. 24:9–11

Moses stays 40 days on Mt. Sinai. Ten commandment tablets given. Pattern for the tabernacle given. Exod. 24:12; 32:15

Day 16 Exod. 34:2

Eighth ascent and descent of Mt. Sinai by Moses. Renew covenant with nation. Second ten commandment tablets given. Second forty-day stay on Mt. Sinai for Moses. Exod. 34:2–29

Third Month

Day 1 First ascent and descent of Mt. Sinai by Moses. If people obedient, will be a holy nation. Exod. 9:3–7

People agree to be obedient. Exod 19:8

Second ascent and descent of Mt. Sinai by Moses. Moses commanded to sanctify the people. Exod 19:8–14

Day 3 Exod. 19:16

Third ascent and descent of Mt. Sinai by Moses. God fears people may come too close to Mt. Sinai. Exod. 19:20–25

People hear God speak the 10 commandments. Exod. 20:1–20 Deut 5:22

Fourth ascent and descent of Mt. Sinai by Moses. Civil law for the nation given. Exod 20:21–24

People agree to obey all God spoke to Moses. Exod. 24:3

Fourth Month

Day 15 Exod 32:30

Seventh ascent and descent of Mt. Sinai by Moses. Moses speaks to God about the people's sin. Exod. 32:31–34

Moses sets up a tabernacle outside the camp, not the worship tabernacle yet to be built. Exod. 33:7

	First Month	Second Month	Third Mor...
		11th mo., 11th day	11th mo., 29th day
		10th mo.	10th mo.
			14th day

Second year, first month, days 1–7 Moses sets up the tabernacle Exod 40:2, 17, after seven-months-three-day construction period. Seven days of consecration of priest and sanctifying of the tabernacle. Exod. 29:36, 37; 40:9–15; Lev 8:33; Num. 7:1. Beginning of 12 days of altar dedication. Num. 7

Day 12 Altar dedication complete.

Day 13 Tribe of Levi consecrated Num. 8:5–26

Day 14 Second passover. Num. 9:1–14

First Month

Day 8 Two sons of Aaron die. Lev 10:1–2

Timeline of the Exodus and Wilderness Journey

Time span from the Exodus

| 1 yr, 15th day | 1 yr, 1 mo, 5th day | 1 yr, 1 mo, 23rd day |

Time span from arrival at Mt. Sinai

| 11th month | 11th month, 20th day |

Second Month	Third Month	Fourth Month	Fifth Month	Sixth Month
Second year, Day 1 — First numbering. Num. 1:1, 46	**Day 8** — Arrive at Kadesh after eighteen-day journey; eleven-day delay Num. 12:15, seven-day delay Num. 1:2, twelve spies sent to spy out the land. Num. 3:17		**Day 19** — False repentance of nation. Num. 14:40	
	Day 20 — Depart from Mt. Sinai fifty days after tabernacle set up. Num. 10:11		Thirty-eight years wandering after about a one-year stay at Kadesh. Deut 1:46, 2:14	
			Day 18 — Return of spies after forty days. Num. 3:25 Congregation refused to enter Promised Land. Num. 4:1-4	

First Month	Second Month	...	Fifth Month	Sixth Month	Seventh M
Fortieth year — Second time at Kadesh. Stayed here less than four mo. Miriam dies. Num. 20:1			**Fortieth year, fifth month, day 1** — Aaron dies at Mt. Hor. Fourty years from the Exodus. Num. 33:38; Deut 2:7		

Time span from the Exodus

| | 40th year, 11th month, 25th day |
| | 40th year, 10th month, 10th day |

Time span from arrival at Mt. Sinai

| | 40th year, 1st month, 10th day |

Time span from setting up of tabernacle

Time span from departure from Mt. Sinai

| | 39th year, 10th month, 20th day |

Eleventh Month	Twelfth Month	First Month	Second Month	Third
Fortieth year, eleventh month, day 1 — Moses speaks all the Book of Deuteronomy. Deut. 1:3 Moses dies. Deut. 34:5 Nation mourns thirty days for Moses. Deut. 34:8		**Forty-first year, first month, day 1** — Two spies sent to spy land. Josh. 2:1		
		Day 10 — Crossing of the Jordan. Josh. 4:19		

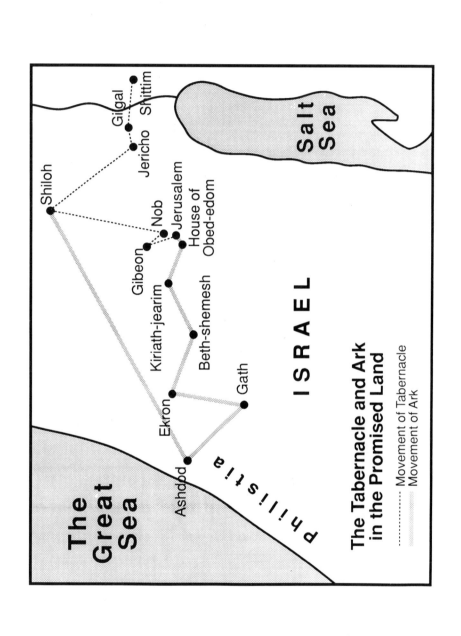

Chronological Chart of Tabernacle Locations After Entry into Canaan

Movement of ark and explanation	Crossing of the Jordan. Tabernacle at Gilgal five years.	Tabernacle set up at Shiloh		Tabernacle at Shiloh 470 years Shiloh destroyed, ark captured		Tabernacle at Nob Nob destroyed	Tabernacle at Gibeon	Tabernacle taken to Jerusalem
Periods	Events of the Book of Joshua		Judges	Samuel as judge	Saul as king	David as king	Solomon as king
Length of Time	25 years		450 years	40 years	40 years 10 20 30 40	40 years 7	40 years 4 12
Movement of tabernacle and explanation				Ark captured seven mo. by Philistines Ark short time at Beth-shemesh Ark at Kiriath-jearim for 87 years		Ark at house of Obed-edom three mo. Ark placed in the tabernacle David made at Jerusalem about seventh year of his reign	Ark placed in holy of holies in Solomon's temple in twelfth year of his reign

The Material and Construction of the Tabernacle

"And let them make me a sanctuary; that I may dwell among them" (Exod. 25:8).

The tabernacle under construction

Instructions for the building of the tabernacle are found in Exodus 25–30, whereas Exodus 35–40 records the actual construction of the tabernacle. As stated earlier, the instructions were spoken to Moses during the sixth of eight ascents of Mount Sinai.

It is worthy to note that the instructions were graphic and complete. Nothing was left to the discretion of Moses. Indeed, Moses was to make everything "after the pattern of the tabernacle, and the pattern of all the instruments thereof, even so shall ye make it" (Exod. 25:9). In Exodus 25:9; 25:40, and Hebrews 8:5, the Hebrew and Greek words for "pattern" is translated to "model

41

for imitation." This indicates that Moses saw an actual tabernacle. Apparently God felt an example was necessary to augment his instructions for it was Moses' solemn duty to give the final approval that the tabernacle was made according to the pattern.

The project got underway on Mount Sinai when God instructed Moses to appoint two men, Bezaleel and Aholiab, as the chief overseers of the construction. Of Bezaleel, God said, "I have filled him with the spirit of God, in wisdom, and in understanding, and in knowledge, and in all manner of workmanship" (Exod. 31:3; 35:31). Aholiab, who was to assist Bezaleel (Exod. 31:6; 35:34–35; 38:23) and all the workers were granted special wisdom to accomplish their tasks (Exod. 36:1–2). Although there is no record of how many workers labored under the guidance of Bezaleel and Aholiab, the number was probably great, since the tabernacle was completed in seven months.

That the construction of the tabernacle was a result of planning and forethought is self-evident, but it is particularly remarkable to note that God, in his incomparable providence, began making provisions for the materials some 400 years earlier. This is prophesied in Genesis 15:13–14:

> And he said unto Abram, Know of a surety that thy seed shall be a stranger in a land that is not theirs, and shall serve them; and they shall afflict them four hundred years; and also that nation, whom they shall serve, will I judge: and afterward shall they come out with great substance.

Much of the tabernacle was constructed from that substance.

God addressed the subject again when he called Moses to deliver the children of Israel out of Egypt (Exod. 3). In verses 21 and 22 of that chapter, God told Moses to have the Israelites "borrow" from the Egyptians jewels of silver and gold and raiment. Moses doubted the Egyptians would cooperate (Exod. 4:1), but the seemingly relentless plagues and the sudden death of the firstborn softened the resolve of the Egyptians (Exod. 11:3; 12:36). The beleaguered Egyptians probably gave begrudgingly, but they certainly felt it was in their best interest to supply all that the Israelites had asked. Thus the material for the construction of the tabernacle was the fruit of the spoils. Although it was a glorious moment for the Israelites, the spoiling of the Egyptians has often been criticized. There was no deceit involved, however. The Hebrew word *shaal* is translated "borrow" only six out of 168 times it is used (Exod. 3:22; 11:2; 12:35). The context of these verses strongly suggest that the translation "ask" is best, particularly since it is obvious that there was no intention of returning the spoils.

Paradoxically, God then asked the children of Israel to give the spoils to him (Exod. 35:4–5). Unlike the Egyptians, the Israelites gave from a grateful heart. Through this freewill offering everyone was able to participate in the construction of the tabernacle. All who felt compelled to give did so abundantly; for, after a few days Moses commanded that no additional material be brought. There was more than enough material for the tabernacle (Exod. 36:3–7).

Material

A considerable variety of materials was used in the construction of the tabernacle. Exodus 25:3–7, the original proclamation by God on Mount Sinai, and Exodus 35:4–9, when Moses instructed the nation to bring the materials, lists the materials. They can be separated into six categories: metal, fabric, skin, wood, oil, spices, and stone.

Metals

Gold, silver, and brass, the three kinds of metals used in the construction of the tabernacle, are recognized for their malleability, an essential quality considering these metals were used primarily to overlay wood. Metals were the most costly materials used in the construction of the tabernacle. Their combined value on today's market would be estimated at $12,896,960 and their combined weight was 18,916 pounds. The shekel and the talent, which were units of weight and not coins, were the conventional currency used by the Hebrews at this time. Coins were not in common use until a later date. I use 220 grains for a shekel and 3,000 shekels (Exod. 38:25–26) for a talent, which puts the weight of a talent at ninety-four pounds.

Gold was the most precious metal used in the construction of the tabernacle. A total of twenty-nine talents, 730 shekels was used for the pillars, walls, and furniture of the sanctuary (Exod.

38:24). This amount of gold weighs 2,757 pounds and would be valued at $12,062,874 at $300 a troy ounce.

Unlike the other metals, silver was not obtained from the freewill offering of the congregation. It was produced from a special registration tax of one-half shekel levied on all men who met the age requirements for military service and were thus numbered (Exod. 30:11–16). It is a matter of controversy that the number of men who gave one-half shekel at this time (603,550, Exod. 38:26) agrees exactly with the numbering of the nation eight months later (603,550 Num. 2:32). Although it seems improbable that the figure would remain unchanged, there seems to be no satisfactory explanation for the coincidence.

The 100 talents, 1,775 shekels of silver collected were used for sockets, chapiters, hooks, and fillets (Exod. 38:25–28). This is an enormous amount of silver, 9,484 pounds. At $6 a troy ounce, it would be worth $829,881. One talent was used for each of the ninety-six wall sockets and the four sockets of the pillars in the sanctuary, which left 1,775 shekels of silver, or fifty-six pounds to make the hooks, fillets, and overlay of the chapiters for the pillars of the outer court. It is doubtful that the fifty-six pounds of silver would be sufficient to make solid silver fillets and hooks for the sixty pillars of the court. Therefore, although it is not stated in scripture, these too were probably overlaid as the chapiters (Exod. 38:28).

The word *brass* used in the King James Version text is best translated copper. Brass, which is an alloy of copper and zinc, was not developed until a much later date. The reference was probably to copper or possibly bronze, which was used at this time, but Deuteronomy 8:9 states that the metal was dug from the ground, which indicates copper, a raw metal, rather than bronze, an alloy of copper and tin.

The amount of copper (brass) used was seventy talents, 2,400 shekels, or 6,675 pounds (Exod. 38:29). At 63¢ a pound, this amount of copper is worth $4205. Copper (brass) was used for the sockets of the sixty court pillars, the sockets of the five pillars of the sanctuary, the pins, and the brazen altar (Exod. 38:30–31).

Although the laver and its foot were made of copper (brass), the metal did not come from the original freewill offering of the congregation but from the mirrors of the women who assembled at the door of the court (Exod. 38:8). Scholars surmise that these women, who were not part of a divinely established order, were either there out of curiosity or possibly they had dedicated themselves to fasting and prayer at the tabernacle. A similar class of women is mentioned in 1 Samuel 2:22 and Luke 2:37.

Fabrics

There were two kinds of fabrics used in the construction of the tabernacle, fine linen and woven goat hair.

The Egyptians were well-known for their fine linen. Amazingly, Egyptian linen is considered to be of a better quality than modern machine-produced linen. It is certain that during their long captivity in Egypt, the children of Israel learned how to manufacture fine linen from the flax plant. Their skills in this trade were put to use, for fine linen was used throughout the tabernacle; the outer-court curtain, the gate, the two veils, the ten curtain coverings, and the priests' garments. Except for the outer-court curtains, all of the linen used in the tabernacle were of three colors: red, blue, and purple.

The woven goat hair fabric was used only for the eleven curtain coverings of the tabernacle proper. They are often mistakenly described as white, no doubt because common Western goats are white. In the East, however, goats are black, white being uncommon. The Bedouins, a nomadic Arabic people, continue to make their tents from the black, woven goat hair common in the East. There is reference to the black tents of the Bedouins or Kedars in the Song of Solomon. An important characteristic of goat hair is that it swells when it becomes wet, thus making a water-tight covering.

Skins

In just two verses we find all the information given about the two kinds of skins used for the tabernacle which were ram and badger skin (Exod. 26:14; 36:19). Ram skin was the skin of a male sheep, dyed red and used for the second covering of the tabernacle proper. Badger skin was used for the outermost covering of the tabernacle proper. It has been debated as to what animal is meant by the badger, because of the seven species of badgers found worldwide; none are indigenous to Egypt or the Sinai. The derivation of the word *badger* would indicate that it was a marine animal. Several other animals have been suggested: dugong, seal, and porpoise. Seals and dugongs were common in the Red Sea, and porpoises were common in the Nile River and Mediterranean Sea during this period. Badger skin was also used for shoe leather (Ezek. 16:10), probably because of its durability, a reason why it may have been chosen for the outside covering of the tabernacle proper. Since the dugong, an aquatic mammal similar to our manatee, is still used for shoe leather by the Bedouins, this seems a likely choice.

Because of the value of badger skin as shoe leather, it must have been difficult to give up as a freewill offering. Thus, this seemingly unimportant offering became a demonstration of the Israelites' confidence in God. We find their faith is rewarded in Deuteronomy 29:5, which says that during their forty years in the wilderness, "their shoes waxed not old upon their feet."

Wood

Only one kind of wood was used in the tabernacle, shittim wood, which came from the acacia tree commonly found in the Sinai Peninsula. The acacia tree should not be confused with the North American acacia, which is of another order and thus unrelated. Shittim wood is a hard, yellow-brown, fine-grained wood that turns darker, almost black, with age. Its durability is characterized in the Septuagint where it is translated "incorruptible wood." It was used for the boards, pillars, chapiters, ark, incense altar, table of shewbread, and altar of burnt offering. Because the acacia tree is not a large tree it is obvious that the larger wooden items, such as boards and pillars, could not have been of one piece and were, therefore, formed of joined pieces. All of the shittim wood was overlaid with gold, silver, or brass, with the exception of the wood used for the sixty pillars of the outer court.

Oils and Spices

The oil and spices mentioned in Exodus 25:6 were used for the light of the candlestick, holy anointing oil, and sweet incense. The following oil and spices were used in making holy anointing oil (Exod. 30:22–23): olive oil, myrrh, cinnamon, calamus, and cassia.

Olive oil is a pale-yellow to yellow-green oil of the olive tree, which grows abundantly in Palestine. Only the purest olive oil was used. The oil was also used for the light of the candlestick

(Exod. 27:20 and Lev. 24:2), and the holy anointing oil (Exod. 30:22–23).

Myrrh is a yellow to reddish-brown, aromatic bitter-gum resin from the stem of the balsam bush found in Arabia and Africa. Only pure myrrh, or that which comes spontaneously from the bark, was used.

Cinnamon oil comes from the inner rind of the cinnamon tree, which grows in Ceylon and islands of the Indian Ocean. The oil derived from this spice is pale yellow.

Calamus is a spice which comes from the root of the sweet cane, which grows in Arabia and India. From the calamus a yellow aromatic oil can be extracted.

Cassia is another spice which comes from the aromatic inner bark of a shrub that resembles the cinnamon tree. It grows in various locations in the East.

Holy anointing oil was made from combinations of myrrh, cinnamon, calamus, cassia, and olive oil in the following proportions: myrrh, 500 shekels or sixteen pounds; cinnamon, 250 shekels or eight pounds; calamus, 250 shekels or eight pounds; cassia, 500 shekels or sixteen pounds; and one hin or six quarts of olive oil. The holy anointing oil was more than a mixture of the ingredients mentioned. It is easy to see that forty-eight pounds of dry spices mixed with only six quarts of olive oil could not produce a liquid ointment. Therefore, it was compounded after the art of the apothecary (Exod. 30:25). Most likely the amounts for these four spices were actually used for the extracting of their oils, which were then added to the olive oil. The holy anointing oil was used to consecrate persons or things to God, and its use was prohibited for any other purpose.

The following spices were used in making sweet incense (Exod. 30:34–38): stacte, onyche, galbanum, and frankincense.

Stacte is probably the gum of the storax tree found in the East.

Onyche is a spice obtained from the opercula of a shellfish found in the Red Sea, probably of the family Strombus. When it is burned, it produces a strong odor that increases the fragrance of other perfumes.

Galbanum is a yellow to green or brown, aromatic bitter-gum resin extracted from a shrub that grows in Arabia, Persia, India, and Africa. Although its odor is disagreeable, it enables the incense to retain its fragrance longer. It also had medicinal value.

Frankincense is a white-to-yellow, aromatic gum resin which contains a volatile oil. It comes from a tree that grows in Arabia and India. Frankincense is regarded as a precious perfume. It was also used separately with the meat offerings (Lev. 2:1–2) and the shewbread offering (Lev. 24:7).

Sweet incense was made from equal parts of these four spices: stacte, onycha, galbanum, and frankincense. It was compounded after the art of the apothecary and, like the holy anointing oil, was prohibited for private use. Sweet incense was used only at the golden incense altar each morning and evening, and annually on the Day of Atonement when it was burned before the ark. The term "strange incense" in Exodus 30:9 refers to any incense not mixed properly. Sweet incense was stored in the holy place where some believe it was kept in the spoons or small censers at the table of shewbread, since the table of shewbread was the only furniture mentioned having spoons (Exod. 25:29) used to hold incense (Num. 7:86).

Stones

Twelve different stones were part of the material offered for use at the tabernacle (see page 70). They were part of the special garments for the high priest. A list of the stones is found in Exodus 28:9; 17–20. Each of the twelve stones on the high priest's breastplate had a name of one of the twelve tribes engraved on it. Also, on the shoulders of the robe of the ephod were two onyx stones, each engraved with six names of the twelve tribes according to their birth (Exod. 28:10).

There is some scholarly objection to the use of several of these stones on the basis that ancient engravers did not possess lapidary tools capable of cutting some of the harder stones. However, we must not forget that God filled Bezaleel and Aholiab with his Spirit and gave them special ability to make everything for the tabernacle. This included the cutting of stones (Exod. 35:33). The value of the stones is difficult to estimate because their size, color, and quality is unknown. Assuming that each stone weighed about two carats and was of the best quality, at today's prices their combined value would be close to $175,000.

Two other items, the urim and thummim, although in scripture not specifically described or commanded to be made, were probably stones. They were used by the high priest in an unknown

The Material and Construction of the Tabernacle

Urim and thummim

way to discern the will of God in important matters (Num. 27:21). As such, they were kept in a pouch under the high priest's breastplate (Exod. 28:30). The method of obtaining an answer may have been by the casting of lots, because the Hebrew word *lot* originally meant a small stone. This would support the theory that the stones were marked to indicate a yes or no answer; thus, on removing one from the pouch, the priest would receive an immediate indication of God's will.

The material used for the construction of the tabernacle made it a costly structure. An idea of how costly it would be to build the tabernacle at today's prices is estimated below. The estimates do not include labor for the seven-month construction period, which would significantly increase its cost.

Defining the Three Areas of the Tabernacle

The overall structure of the tabernacle can be divided into two general areas: the court of the tabernacle and the tabernacle proper, which was a tentlike structure divided into two sections called the *holy place* and the *holy of holies*, a phrase often used in

Table 2 **Estimated Present Day Cost to Build the Tabernacle**

Gold	$12,062,874
Silver	829,881
Copper	4,205
Linen	9,000
Goat Hair	5,000
Ram skin	31,500
Badger skin	31,500
Wood	190,000
Oil, spices	no estimate
Stones	175,000
Total:	$13,338,960

modern English Bibles. These two descriptive terms can be confusing (see chart page 71). For instance, the holy of holies is called the most holy (Exod. 26:33, 34 and 1 Chron. 6:49) or holiest (Heb. 9:3, 8; 10:19) but never the holy of holies in the King James Version. In Leviticus 16:2, it is called the holy place, but from the context we know this scripture is actually referring to the holy of holies. The same is true in Hebrews 9:12, 25.

The term *holy place* is used correctly but only when the word *place* (King James Version) is in italics as in Exodus 26:33; 38:24 and Leviticus 6:30. Another term used often in the Old Testament for the holy place is sanctuary (Lev. 4:6). Exodus 25:8 and Numbers 3:31 indicate it was also used to designate the tabernacle proper. In the New Testament the holy place is called the sanctuary (Heb. 8:2, 9:1–2; 13:11).

The outer court is usually designated by the word *court*, but it is sometimes called the holy place. It can be distinguished as the outer court when the word *place* is not in italics as in Leviticus 6:16; 7:6; Exodus 29:31. (An exception to this is found in Lev. 10:18.) In Numbers 18:10, the outer court is called the most holy place because it was most holy, compared to the rest of the camp. Noting these differences is necessary to understand the ceremonies and offerings that took place at the tabernacle.

Court of the Tabernacle

The court of the tabernacle (Exod. 27:9–19; 38:9–20) was the largest single area of the tabernacle. It measured 100 cubits (208 feet) in length and fifty cubits (104 feet) in width. For the calcu-

The Material and Construction of the Tabernacle 51

Court of the tabernacle

lations in this book, I use twenty-five inches to a cubit. Although the ancient cubit varied from eighteen to twenty-five inches, a cubit is represented in the Great Pyramid of Egypt as twenty-five inches. This is believed to be the standard cubit used by Egyptians, who were probably the first to standardize it. Since the Israelites began construction of the tabernacle only four months after the Exodus, it seems likely that they used the Egyptian cubit, one with which they were familiar.

The court itself was surrounded by a linen curtain supported by sixty pillars made of shittim wood. Each pillar had a copper (brass) socket base and was capped with a wooden chapiter overlaid with silver. Connecting each pillar was a fillet or rod from which the linen curtains hung. Hooks were used to hold the fillet to the pillars and to tie the cords, which were also tied to copper (brass) pins driven into the ground. Although the height of the pillars is not given, they were, no doubt, as high as the curtains, which were five cubits (ten feet, four inches) high.

Door of the Tabernacle

There was one entrance into the court of the tabernacle (Exod. 27:16 and 38:18), a gate commonly called the door of the taber-

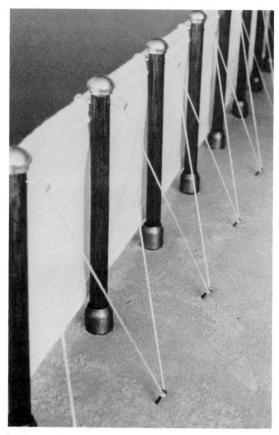
Linen curtain

nacle which was always to face east (Num. 3:38). Other names used for this entrance are gate of the court (Exod. 27:16), court gate (Exod. 38:15) and door of the court (Exod. 35:17). This entrance should not be confused with the outer veil of the holy place, which is called the "hanging for the door of the tabernacle," and other similar terms incorporating the distinguishing word "hanging," as in Numbers 3:25; 4:25 and Exodus 35:15; 36:37; 39:38; 40:5, 28. The beautifully ornate door of the court was twenty cubits wide (forty-one feet, six inches) with needlework of blue, red, and purple.

Inside the court were only two pieces of furniture, the brazen altar and the laver.

The Material and Construction of the Tabernacle 53

Door of the tabernacle

Altar

The altar (Exod. 27:1–8; 38:1–7), as it is commonly called, was also called the brazen altar (Exod. 38:30; 39:39) the altar of burnt offering (Exod. 30:28; 31:9). It was located in the court, directly in front of the gate (Exod. 40:29). The altar was the largest single piece of furniture of the tabernacle. It was square, measuring five cubits (ten feet, four inches) long and three cubits (six feet, three inches) high. It was made of shittim wood overlaid with copper (brass). Wood overlaid with copper so that it is airtight is absolutely fireproof.

On each of its corners was a horn, which seems to have had no definite purpose, although some believe the sacrificial animals were tied to them because of Psalm 118:27. This is not known to have been practiced since sacrificial animals were already killed and quartered when they were brought to the altar (Lev. 1:11, 12; 6:25; 7:2). The word used for sacrifice in Psalm 118:27 means a festal sacrifice, the sacrifice at one of the national feasts. Perhaps because of the large number of animals offered at the feast, some of them were tied to the horns before being sacrificed.

Altar

There was also a copper (brass) grate in the altar, on which the wood and animals to be sacrificed were placed (Lev. 1:12). This grate was a little lower than the height of the compass or middle of the altar. The word *compass* means rim. It was apparently a shelf that completely circumvented the altar as a platform on which the priest performed the sacrifices. Aaron is said to have come down from the altar (Lev. 9:22), because the compass would be about three feet up the side of the altar. It is assumed that there was a slope of earth up to the compass to serve as a support and to comply with Exodus 20:26, which forbade steps to the altar. Some have incorrectly assumed that the instructions concerning altars in Exodus 20:24–26 also apply to the brazen altar (see chapter 6, page 119).

Several utensils were used to aid the priests in their work at the altar. These were all made of copper (brass) and included the following: ash pans to catch the ashes and sacrifices and to carry them to a clean place outside the camp (Lev. 6:10–11), shovels for the removal of the ashes, basins to catch the blood of the slain animals, fleshhooks to place the various parts of the animals sacrificed in their proper order on the altar (Lev. 1:8; 1 Sam. 2:13), firepans, which are rendered snuffdishes in Exodus 25:38 and

The Material and Construction of the Tabernacle 55

Grate of the altar

37:23, and censers in Leviticus 10:1 and Numbers 16:6 which were used to transport the burning coals from the brazen altar to the candlestick and incense altar in the holy place. Firepans were probably used in conjunction with fueling the perpetual fire of the brazen altar when traveling (Lev. 6:13). Leviticus 10:1 and Ezekiel 8:11 indicate that each priest had his own firepan.

Laver

Between the altar and the outer veil of the tabernacle proper stood the laver (Exod. 30:17–21; 38:8), a large wash bowl used by the priests to wash their hands and feet before ministering at the altar or inside the holy place. It was also used to wash the animals that were sacrificed (Lev. 1:9). You will note from Exodus 38:8; 29–31 that the laver was not made from the copper (brass) taken in the congregational freewill offering but was made from the mirrors of the women who assembled at the door of the tabernacle. Unlike the altar, the layer was solid copper (brass) and had a foot or stand as a base.

References to the laver, unlike the other furniture of the tabernacle, are lacking in detail. For instance, there is no mention

Laver

of any accompanying utensils, but most likely bowls were used for washing. Also, the other furniture had either a bar or staves used to carry them, but none is mentioned with the laver. There is no mention of a covering for travel and, unlike the other furniture, no size or shape is indicated.

The Tabernacle Proper

The tent portion of the tabernacle was divided into two sections, the holy place and the holy of holies, which together measured sixty-two feet, five inches long and twenty-five feet wide. It consisted of an earthen floor (Num. 5:17) and a ceiling made of a four-layer covering that was probably peaked. The structure utilized three solid walls, as in a permanent structure. The larger parts, such as the walls and pillars, were made of light wood with a thin layer of heavier metals. This design served to make it strong, yet light and easily portable. The portability of the tabernacle was its most unique and practical design characteristic, for it was to be moved many times before its usefulness ceased.

The Four-Layer Covering

Protecting the tabernacle were four coverings: badger skin, ram skin, goat hair, and linen (Exod. 26:1–14 and Exod. 36:8–19).

Tabernacle proper

The badger skin (Exod. 26:14; 36:19), because of its apparent durability, was selected as the outermost covering of the four-layer covering of the tabernacle proper. This layer took the punishment of the blistering rays of the sun in the desert climate of the Sinai, as well as the rain and snow of the Promised Land. The badger's tough, undyed skin was probably unattractive. Although no size is given for this covering, it was certainly larger than those under it. It is estimated to be as large as 6,000 square feet, taking approximately 1,000 to 1,500 skins.

Under the badger skin, the second covering was made from ram skin dyed red (Exod. 26:14 and 36:19). Although no size is given, the entire covering was probably slightly smaller than the badger skin.

The third covering was made of eleven individual goat-hair curtains which measured thirty cubits (sixty-two feet, five inches) long and four cubits (eight feet, four inches) wide (Exod. 26:7–13 and Exod. 36:14–18). Joined together, these eleven curtains made a covering sixty-two feet, five inches long and ninety-one feet, six inches wide. The covering was divided into two sections, the front half being made of six curtains and the back half being made of five curtains. Along each inside edge of the two halves were fifty loops connected by fifty copper (brass) taches or hooks. This assembly formed the complete goat-hair covering. This design made the two sections easier to transport, an important consideration. Although scripture does not mention taches for the badger- and ram-skin coverings, as it does for the linen covering, these too may have incorporated taches.

The goat-hair covering is the only covering with specific information about its placement over the tabernacle. The sixth curtain of the front half was to be doubled in the front of the tabernacle (Exod. 26:9). It is not clear whether this means it was dropped over the front of the tabernacle or folded back under the other coverings. The last curtain of the back half of the covering hung over the back wall one half of its width or about four feet. The covering hung one cubit (twenty-five inches) over each side of the tabernacle (Exod. 26:13). Considering this information, it would be impossible for the tabernacle to have a flat roof as many have surmised. Instead of the covering hanging well over the sides, it must have been held up by the nine pillars of the tabernacle to meet the biblical requirements and thus form a raised or peaked roof (see Pillars and Veils, page 59).

The fine-linen covering (Exod. 26:1–6; 36:8–13) was the only covering that could be seen from inside the tabernacle proper. The fine-linen covering was colorfully embroidered in blue, purple, and red with the design of cherubim. The covering was made of ten individual curtains, each twenty-eight cubits (fifty-eight feet, three inches) long and four cubits (eight feet, three inches) wide. Joined together, they made a covering fifty-eight feet, three inches long and eighty-three feet, three inches wide. Like the goat-hair covering, this covering was divided into two halves. The inside edge of each half had fifty blue-colored loops connected by fifty gold taches.

Walls

The three walls of the tabernacle proper (Exod. 26:15–30; 36:20–34) were made of forty-eight boards of shittim wood overlaid with gold. Twenty boards were used for the north and south walls and eight boards were used for the west or back wall. Each board was ten cubits (twenty feet, eight inches) high and one and one-half cubits (three feet, one and one-half inches) wide. Their thickness is not given, but the Talmud says they were one cubit thick.

Although Exodus 26:23–24, which describes the two corner boards of the back wall, is not easily understood, it is generally believed that the back wall joined on the outside edges of the two side walls and not on their inside edges. This would make the tabernacle sixty-two feet, five inches long and twenty-five feet wide.

Each board had two tenons, or small wooden pegs, which fitted them into silver sockets or bases. There were ninety-six sockets, two for each board. Each socket weighed a talent (Exod. 38:27).

There were also five bars of shittim wood overlaid with gold for each wall. They were used to connect the boards to one another for additional strength. Four of the bars ran the full length of a wall through golden rings attached to each board. The fifth bar went through the center of each board the full length of a wall (Exod. 26:28; 36:33).

The unique design of the walls of the tabernacle made it a sturdy structure capable of being quickly and easily assembled and disassembled.

Pillars and Veils

Two sets of pillars were used in the tabernacle, each with its own veil (Exod. 26:31–37; 36:35–38). The first set consisted of five pillars, which had chapiters of shittim wood overlaid with gold. They were placed at the entrance to the holy place at the front of the tabernacle proper. Each pillar had copper (brass) sockets and gold hooks for the outer veil to hang on. Several times in scripture the outer veil is called the "door of the tabernacle" as is the gate of the court (see door of the tabernacle). The outer veil was made of linen with needlework designs in blue, purple, and scarlet.

badger-skin covering

ram-skin covering

goat-hair covering

fine-linen covering

The four-layer covering

The Material and Construction of the Tabernacle 61

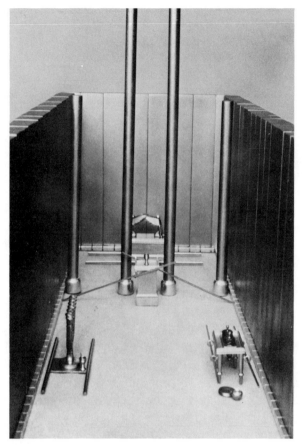

Walls of the tabernacle

The second set of pillars consisted of four pillars of shittim wood, overlaid with gold but without chapiters. Their sockets weighed one talent each and were made of silver instead of copper (brass)(Exod. 38:27). Each pillar had a hook from which the veil to the holy of holies hung. This veil is called the second veil in Hebrews 9:3. This veil was woven in blue, purple, and scarlet with the design of cherubim. It corresponds to the veil of the temple that was torn from top to bottom when Christ died. It served as the dividing line between the holy place and the holy of holies and was located directly under the taches of the linen and goat hair coverings (Exod. 26:33). This indicates that the four inner pillars were about forty feet from the entrance, which corresponds to Jewish tradition.

Walls showing the bars

Because no height is given for any of the pillars, many have assumed that the roof of the tabernacle was flat and flush with the walls. This is not a correct conclusion. Because the goat-hair covering was to hang exactly one cubit (twenty-five inches) over the sides of the walls, it is necessary for the pillars to extend above the walls to take up the slack of the goat-hair covering. This necessitates a roof higher than the sides of the tabernacle; one most likely peaked to some degree (see page 72). This would make the center pillar about forty-seven feet high.

Candlestick

Located on the south side of the holy place was the candlestick (Exod. 25:31–40; 27:20–21; 30:7, 8; 37:17–24; Lev. 24:1–4; Num. 8:1–4) or, more properly, the lamp. It was made from a talent of pure gold and was a beaten work, having one center shaft and six branches with bowls, knops, and flowers. Its size is not mentioned, but tradition has established it to be about five feet tall. Although the knops and flowers of the candlestick were merely ornamental, the bowls did serve to hold olive oil and wicks or, as Exodus 25:37 suggests, they may have been used only as holders for lamps.

The Material and Construction of the Tabernacle

Pillars and veils

Three utensils, golden tongs, snuffdishes, and oil vessels, are mentioned in association with the candlestick (Exod. 25:38 and Num. 4:9). Tongs were used to clean and trim the wicks. The word used for snuffdishes is the same as the word used for censers elsewhere; therefore, they were probably used to hold coals from the brazen altar. The oil vessels were apparently used as containers for the pure olive oil.

A bar (Num. 4:10), instead of a stave, was used for carrying the candlestick. A bar was a carrier for the items which did not utilize rings for staves as a permanent part of its construction. Other instruments of ministry used in the sanctuary were carried on bars (Num. 4:12).

Second set of pillars and second veil

Table of Shewbread

Located on the north side of the holy place was the table of shewbread (Exod. 25:23–30, 37:10–16; Lev. 24:5–9). It was made of shittim wood overlaid with gold, and was two cubits (fifty inches) long and one cubit (twenty-five inches) wide, and one and one-half cubits (three feet, one and one-half inches) tall.

On each corner were gold rings for the two shittim wood staves overlaid with gold for carrying the table. On its top were two crowns or borders, one on the outside edge of the table, the other a hand's breadth in, to hold the shewbread in position. The shewbread was kept in two rows or stacks with six cakes in each row (Lev. 24:6). The word *row* in Leviticus 24:6 should probably be

Candlestick

translated "stacks," because it is not the same word used to designate side-by-side rows as in Exodus 28:17–20 and elsewhere. It would be physically impossible for twelve loaves of bread to be placed individually side by side on a table of this dimension, since the amount of flour needed for each loaf (two-tenths deal or a gallon) would make them about eighteen inches in diameter. On top of each row (stack) was frankincense, which was probably kept in a spoon, because the priest ate the shewbread (Lev. 24:9).

There were several golden utensils kept at the table of shewbread. They included dishes, spoons, bowls, and covers.

The shewbread may have been eaten or mixed in dishes. Spoons used at the table of shewbread held pure frankincense. Because spoons are not mentioned with any other furnishings, it is thought these spoons, used to hold incense (Num. 7:86), were not only kept on the table of shewbread but also used at the incense altar. They were actually small censers capable of holding about a cupped hand of incense. Each weighed ten shekels or about five ounces (Num. 7:86).

Bowls were used to hold the blood used in the holy places, such as the blood used in the priest's or congregation's sin offerings and

Table of shewbread

on the Day of Atonement. Covers were actually jugs or pitchers and were used probably to hold the wine for the drink offering.

Altar of Incense

The altar of incense, or golden altar (Exod. 30:1–10; 37:25–28), was located just in front of the veil to the holy of holies. It was made of shittim wood overlaid with gold and was one cubit (25 inches) long and two cubits (50 inches) high. On opposite corners were two gold rings for shittim wood staves overlaid with gold. Although no utensils are mentioned with the incense altar, we learn from Leviticus 16:12, 13 and Hebrews 9:4 that there was a golden censer on the altar for the burning of the incense. There was also a crown or border around its edge, apparently to keep the golden censer in place, as well as horns on each corner.

Ark and Mercy Seat

The word *ark* refers to the chestlike structure that the mercy seat sat upon, the mercy seat being its lid or cover. Collectively they are called the ark (Exod. 25:10–22; 37:1–9).

The ark was made of shittim wood overlaid with gold, mea-

Altar of incense

suring two and one-half cubits (five feet, two and one-half inches) long, one and one-half cubits (three feet, one and one-half inches) wide and one and one-half cubits high, with a crown or border to secure the mercy seat.

The mercy seat was a solid gold lid of the same dimension as the top of the ark. Located at each of its ends were gold cherubim, with wings stretched over the seat as they faced toward each other and down toward the mercy seat. The amount of gold used for the mercy seat is not given.

The ark had four gold rings, two on each side, which were probably located near its base since the word used for corners (Exod. 25:12) can be translated "feet" as it is in the American

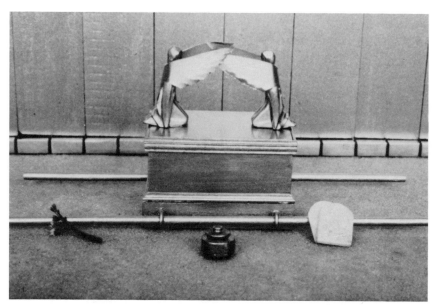

Ark and mercy seat with contents

Standard Version. The rings held two shittim wood staves overlaid with gold. The Israelites were specifically commanded to keep the staves permanently in the rings (Exod. 25:15). The ark contained three items: the golden pot of manna, Aaron's rod that budded, and the tables of the covenant (Heb. 9:4).

Although it is agreed that the ark faced east, the position of the staves is often a subject of disagreement. I believe the staves ran north and south and not east and west, for the following reasons: Exodus 25:12 says they were on the sides and not the ends; only in this position could the cherubim of Solomon's temple cover the ark and staves (1 Kings 8:7); if the staves ran east and west they would interfere with the performance of the high priests on the Day of Atonement.

The Material and Construction of the Tabernacle

Bezaleel makes the ark

Table 3 **Stones of the Breastplate**

Name	Name on Stone (by birth)	Group	Description	Modern Name of Stone
First Row				
Sardus	Reuben	quartz	pale red to deep red, brownish red to yellow brown chalcedony	sard or carnelian
Topaz	Simeon	topaz	yellow, colorless, light red, brown, blue, violet	topaz
Carbuncle	Judah	garnet	deep red, violet red through brownish red to almost black	almandite garnet
Second Row				
Emerald	Levi	beryl	green	emerald
Sapphire	Dan	corundum	blue, pink, green, violet, yellow	sapphire
Diamond	Naphtali	diamond	colorless, blue, green, yellow, brown, red, black	diamond
Third Row				
Ligure	Gad	zircon	orange, yellow, red, brown	perhaps the jacinth or hyacinth
Agate	Asher	quartz	white, gray, brown, reddish, colored layers, chalcedony	agate
Amethyst	Issachar	quartz	purple, violet	amethyst
Fourth Row				
Beryl	Zebulon	beryl	light green	beryl
Onyx	Joseph	quartz	white and black, colored bands, chalcedony	onyx
Jasper	Benjamin	quartz	ocher yellow to chestnut brown, banded in red-yellow or red-green stripes, variegated, chalcedony	jasper

Areas of the Tabernacle

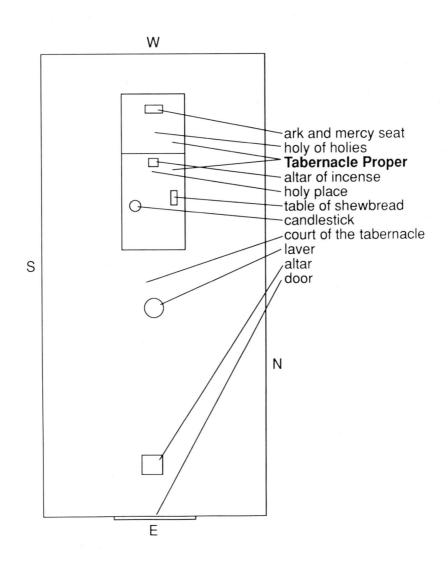

Tabernacle Roof

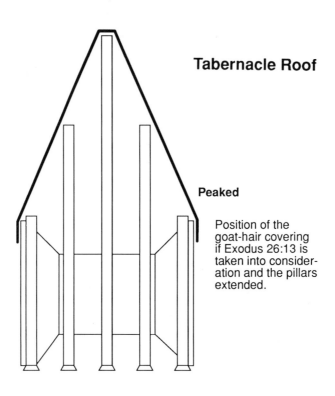

Peaked

Position of the goat-hair covering if Exodus 26:13 is taken into consideration and the pillars extended.

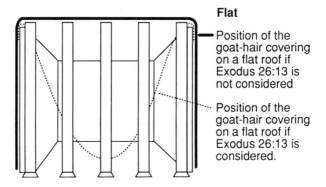

Flat

Position of the goat-hair covering on a flat roof if Exodus 26:13 is not considered

Position of the goat-hair covering on a flat roof if Exodus 26:13 is considered.

Levitical Priesthood

"And take thou unto thee Aaron thy brother, and his sons with him, from among the children of Israel, that he may minister unto me in the priest's office" (Exod. 28:1).

The high priest

It is interesting to note that the term *Levitical priesthood* is not found in the Old Testament, and it is found in the New Tes-

73

tament only once (Heb. 7:11). Strictly speaking, this term refers only to the high priest and the priests, the sons of Aaron; although, in another sense, it applies to the rest of the tribe of Levi because of their appointment as ministers to the priests and their work at the tabernacle (see chart page 95).

The Book of Hebrews has much to say about the high priest as a type of Christ and of his relationship to the tabernacle, its furniture, and its rituals. It would be just as impossible to understand the importance of the tabernacle without understanding the office of the high priest as it would be to understand the gospel without Jesus. It would be a "gospel" without Jesus and that would be no gospel at all. Understanding the office of the high priest is essential in fully realizing the tabernacle as the "gospel" preached to the Israelites.

With the establishment of the Levitical priesthood, the Israelites had a greater revelation of the work of the true high priest, Jesus Christ; however, there had long been men who had served in the capacity of priest. The first priests were merely the heads of families, such as Noah (Gen. 8:20), Job (Job 1:5), Abraham (Gen. 22:3), Isaac (Gen. 26:6–25), or heads of a tribe or nation, such as Melchizedek (Gen. 14:18), Jethro (Exod. 18:12), or Israelite priests (Exod. 19:22, 24), or Balak (Num. 22:40). The institution of the Levitical priesthood initiated major changes in the selection and work of priests.

The Levitical priesthood differed from its precursors in that it was hereditary; only the sons of Aaron could represent God in this capacity, doing away with the ancient privilege of the heads of the families serving as priests. Furthermore, priests of the Levitical priesthood only fulfilled this capacity at the tabernacle, which served to centralize the priesthood. This was to assure that the proper procedures were followed when the nation approached God. It also served as a unifying force within the nation.

It was an office that was greatly venerated. When the two and one half tribes located on the east side of the Jordan River built an altar at the Jordan in seemingly disrespect to the priesthood, the incident almost caused a civil war (Josh. 22:10–19). Why? Because only the priests were to make the offerings and only at the altar of the tabernacle (Lev. 17), which was then at Shiloh. The wisdom of centralized worship for God's people at this time is clearly illustrated after the Israelites were settled in the Promised Land, and the use of high places for idol worship began to be tolerated.

This spirit of divided worship and the accompanying practice of idolatry contributed to the division of the nation. All high places, which were commonly used by heathen nations for idol worship, were to be destroyed (Deut. 12:2). Later, with the division of the nation of Israel, Jeroboam established rival priests and other places of sacrifice in Bethel and Dan that effectively kept many of the northern ten tribes from going to Jerusalem to make their sacrifices (1 Kings 12:28–33), contributing to the destruction of the nation's unity.

The work of the priests under the Levitical priesthood was also more elaborate and ritualistic than the work of the other priests up to this time. As we learn from the Book of Hebrews, it was more meaningful and held a greater significance. This was due to the addition of the tabernacle and the institution of rituals that greatly increased priestly responsibilities. Again from Hebrews, we learn that this also revealed the importance of priests in the role as a type of the reconciliatory ministry of Christ.

To better facilitate our understanding of the Levitical priests and their relationship to the tabernacle, we shall consider their call, their consecration, and their work.

Their Call

To understand how the first high priest, Aaron, and the tribe of Levi were chosen can best be illustrated by a chronological approach. In scripture, neither Aaron nor the tribe of Levi were the first called to this office, but rather the whole nation was called:

> Now therefore, if ye will obey my voice indeed, and keep my covenant, then ye shall be a peculiar treasure unto me above all people: for all the earth is mine: And ye shall be unto me a kingdom of priests, and a holy nation. These are the words which thou shalt speak unto the children of Israel (Exod. 19:5–6).

The establishment of the nation as a kingdom of priests was to be accomplished by sanctifying all firstborn males. This is mentioned several times in scripture (Exod. 13:11–13, 22:29, 34:19

and Num. 18:15), but was first commanded shortly after the death of the Egyptian firstborn at the time of the Exodus. "And the Lord spake unto Moses, saying, sanctify unto me all the firstborn, whatsoever openeth the womb among the children of Israel, both of man and of beast: it is mine" (Exod. 13:1–2).

The sanctification of the firstborn was to serve two purposes. First, it was to be a memorial of the nation's deliverance from Egypt (Exod. 13:14–16 and Num. 3:13). All of the firstborn males were to be redeemed by the payment of five shekels (Num. 18:16), while all firstborn of clean animals were to be the Lord's. Unclean animals could be redeemed with a lamb, but if not redeemed, their necks were to be broken.

The second purpose of separation of the firstborn was to be the means of selecting the priests. With the firstborn of every tribe selected as a minister, it could truly be said the nation of Israel was a kingdom of priests. Although this was God's intention at first, we find the firstborn later being replaced by the males of the tribe of Levi (Num. 3:12, 13, 45; 8:16–19).

The replacement of the firstborn with the Levites is found in Numbers 3:44–48. This action took place after the first census of the nation in which the Levites were not numbered (Num. 1:47–49). The totals were: Gershon with 7,500 (Num. 3:21–22), Kohath with 8,600 (Num. 3:27–28) and Merari with 6,200 (Num. 3:33–34) for a total of 22,300, of which only 8,580 were old enough for the ministry (Num. 4:47–48). This total seems to contradict Numbers 3:39 where it gives the total as 22,000. This 300 difference is usually attributed to a copyist's error, but can probably be better accounted for as the number of firstborn of the Levites since the sanctifying of the firstborn after the Exodus, who were not eligible for redeeming other firstborn.

Also, at this time, the firstborn of Israel from a month old and upward were numbered. The total was 22,273 (Num. 3:42–43). The 273 of the nation which exceeded the 22,000 Levites in the trade were redeemed for five shekels apiece. Moses then gave the money to Aaron and his sons, thus completing the trade and establishing the Levites as the ministering tribe (Num. 3:46–51).

It is natural to wonder why God instituted the Levitical priesthood in favor of a nation of priests. What changed God's mind? In Exodus 19:5, we find the privilege of being a kingdom of priests rested upon their obedience to the covenant. Exodus 32 records the breaking of this covenant when the nation worshiped the golden calf, thus abolishing their privileged position as a kingdom of priests. It was at this time that the Levites were chosen over the firstborn. When Moses came down to the camp from Mt. Sinai and saw Israel's sin, he said, "Who is on the Lord's side? Let him come unto me. And all the sons of Levi gathered themselves together unto him" (Exod. 32:26). They then went out and slew 3,000 who continued to rebel (Exod. 32:28).

One may suppose that their coming to the aid of Moses was due to tribal loyalty, Moses and Aaron being Levites, but in Deuteronomy 33:9, we discover that they kept his covenant. Thus, their zeal was probably from a sincere desire to please God. Because they were unwilling to defile themselves with the worship of the golden calf, God chose them to be the ministers at his sacred dwelling place (Deut. 10:8–9). For Moses said, "consecrate yourselves today to the Lord, even every man upon his son, and upon his brother; that he may bestow upon you a blessing this day" (Exod. 32:29). This exempted the other tribes from ministerial duty until such time that they could exercise this responsibility properly. However, because of their continuous rebellion and disobedience they were never restored.

With the arrival of the New Covenant, the relationship of God's people as a kingdom of priests was reinstated. This is referred to in 1 Peter 2:5, 9 and Revelation 1:6, 5:10 and 20:6 where Christians are called a holy nation and a royal priesthood. Although we do not offer animal sacrifices, we do offer spiritual sacrifices, having a ministry of reconciliation (2 Cor. 5:18). Under the Old Testament economy one could come under a covenant relationship with God simply by being born an Israelite. Under the New Covenant, the only ones who can be in a covenant relationship with God are those born again, those who have the law written on the fleshy tablets of their hearts, and not on the stone of the Old Covenant (2 Cor. 3:3). The difference is the location of God's laws (Heb. 8:10).

We next need to consider how Aaron and his sons were chosen for the priests's office.

The selection of Aaron and his sons as priests (Exod. 28:1) was made while Moses was on Mt. Sinai just before the idolatry of the nation. Therefore, we may assume that the firstborn of the nation, if they had continued faithful, would have been priests also in lieu of the Levites. Presumably the firstborn would have ministered to the priests, Aaron and his sons, and would have provided service at the tabernacle, as became the duty of the Levites (Num. 3:6–7). Therefore, the selection of the firstborn and the later selection of the Levites as their replacements had no bearing on the selection of Aaron and his sons as priests. The choice of Aaron and his sons was very likely an arbitrary selection by God, because we see nothing in scripture that would indicate them as preferable to other Levites, except that Aaron was the brother of Moses and at one time his spokesman (Exod. 4:16).

Although there is nothing of distinction that would qualify Aaron and his sons for the priest's office, the rebellion of Korah certainly confirmed their selection. The rebellion of Korah is found in Numbers 16 and 17. Korah was a Kohathite who led 250 of the princes of the nation against Moses and Aaron, who were also descendants of Kohath as well as Levi (see chart on page 95), saying "Ye take too much upon you, seeing all the congregation are holy" (Num. 16:3). Moses perceived his real intention was seeking the priesthood (Num. 16:10). It was probably jealousy over his relative's position that provoked him to rebel. Moses proposed that they return the next day with censers. Because the whole congregation followed Korah in his rebellion (Num. 16:19), the Lord's wrath was kindled and he would have consumed the whole congregation had it not been for the intercession of Moses and Aaron. Nevertheless, the Lord opened the earth and swallowed Korah and all that belonged to him, while the 250 rebelling princes were destroyed by a fire. The 250 censers of the princes were used to make a covering or encasement for the brazen altar as a memorial that only the seed of Aaron could offer incense before the Lord (Num. 16:36–40).

The next day the congregation again murmured against Moses and Aaron, accusing them of killing the people of the Lord (Num. 16:41). This time the wrath of God consumed 14,700 by plague before Aaron's intercession in the tabernacle availed. This display of divine displeasure was necessary to impress on the nation the sacredness of the priesthood.

Although the judgment against the rebellion of Korah and his followers was sufficient proof of God's sanction of the Aaronic priesthood, God saw fit to provide further proof. This was accomplished by placing twelve rods, each with the name of a tribe on

Levitical Priesthood

it, in the holy of holies. The rod representing the tribe of Levi had Aaron's name on it. God said, "And it shall come to pass, that the man's rod, whom I shall choose, shall blossom: and I will make to cease from me the murmurings of the children of Israel whereby they murmur against you" (Num. 17:5). The next day, when Moses took the rods from the tabernacle, it was Aaron's rod that had budded, bloomed, and yielded almonds. Aaron's rod was then put in the ark as a memorial of God's choice (Heb. 9:4).

There are those who say God is different now; he is not a God of wrath and judgment as he was in the Old Testament, because of all reasons, we live under grace. Do not be deceived: all those who reject God's high priest, Jesus Christ, will suffer a greater punishment (Heb. 10:28–31) than those who rejected only Aaron, who was a type of Christ. With the confirmation of Aaron as high priest, the Lord redefines the office of the priest and the work of the Levites (Numbers 18).

Their Consecration

The word *consecration* means to wholly separate something or someone apart to God and his service. Aaron, the high priest, and his sons were consecrated at a different time and in a different manner than the rest of the tribe of Levi. This indicates a fundamental difference between them: the priests ministered to God, whereas the Levites ministered to the priest.

The first revelation concerning the consecration of the priests is found in Exodus 28 and 29, which was when Moses made his sixth ascent of Mt. Sinai. These two chapters give the details of the garments of the priest and of their consecration rites and offerings. The actual consecration of Aaron and his sons, described in Leviticus 8, did not take place until the eight and one-half months after their selection. The reason for the delay was due mostly to the time needed to construct the tabernacle and the interruption caused by the nation's idolatry.

The consecration of the priests, Aaron and his four sons, lasted for seven days (Lev. 8:35; Exod. 29:37), and began the day the tabernacle was originally set up (Exod. 40:9–15; Lev. 8:10–13). This also coincided with the dedication of the altar, which lasted twelve days (Num. 7:1, 78, 88). It was after the dedication of the altar that the other Levites were consecrated (Num. 8:5–22). Leviticus 8, which describes the actual consecration of the priests, is lacking in some details because this information had been more fully given to Moses earlier (Exod. 28 and 29).

The consecration of Aaron and his four sons can be divided into five distinct acts: presentation, washing, clothing, anointing and offering.

Presentation

Because the ceremony was very important, the whole congregation was called to the door of the tabernacle, or gate (Exod. 29:4; 40:12; Lev. 8:1–5). People would be naturally interested in witnessing this important event because Aaron would now be their only representative to God. The presentation was to impress on the people, as well as the priests, the important responsibility God laid on the priesthood. The priests of Israel could no longer be selected from among any tribe, but would continue only in the Aaronic line as God had confirmed. There could be no excuses when they would later rebel against God's choice.

Washing

After their presentation, Moses brought Aaron and his sons to the laver to be washed (Exod. 29:4; 40:12; Lev. 8:6). This washing speaks of the sinfulness of Aaron and his sons who could not truly represent the sinlessness of Christ. "For the law maketh men high priests which have infirmity," Hebrews 7:28. Their physical cleansing represented the true purity of Christ, and so the washing became a part of their everyday rituals. Thus, they always washed their hands and feet before ministering at the brazen altar or going inside the sanctuary (Exod. 30:20–21).

Clothing

Immediately after their washing, Aaron and his sons were clothed with garments made specifically for their priestly office (Exod. 29:5–9; 39:1–31, 41; 40:13–14; Lev. 8:7–9, 13). Although all of the priestly garments are said to be for glory and beauty (Exod. 28:2, 40), the garments of the high priest were more ornate than those of the priests. The high priest held an exalted position and his attire served to testify of this. His garments clearly identified him as the high priest and inspired the reverence due his position.

There were six items in the priestly ensemble: ephod, girdle, breastplate, robe, mitre and broidered coat (Exod. 28:4) (see page 73).

The ephod was a special garment which only the high priest wore (Exod. 28:5–14; 39:2–7). It was used for the attachment of the breastplate and was woven of fine blue, purple, scarlet, and gold linen. It was worn over the shoulders, hanging down both front and back to the hips. The sides were probably open. The front and back halves were held together at the shoulders by two shoulderpieces. The shoulderpieces consisted of two onyx stones set in encasements of gold and golden rings that attach the breastplate. The names of six of the tribes were engraved on each onyx stone. The ephod signified the responsibility of the high priest in representing the nation before the Lord (Exod. 28:12).

The curious girdle of the ephod for the high priest was woven of fine linen, which was blue, purple, scarlet, and gold, as was the ephod. It held the back and front halves of the ephod together at the waist, below the breastplate. The girdle for the priest was probably white.

The most noticeable and important part of the high priest's garments was the breastplate (Exod. 28:15–30; 39:8–21). It is called the "breastplate of judgment" in Exodus 28:15 because on the backside of the breastplate was a pocket for the urim and thummim, which were used by the high priest to ascertain God's will for the people. The breastplate itself was about nine or ten inches square. Like the ephod and girdle, it was woven of fine linen in blue, purple, scarlet, and gold. Affixed to it were twelve stones, each with a tribe's name engraved upon it (see chart page 70). The stones were arranged in four rows, three to a row in settings of gold. The position of each tribal stone is not given. A gold ring was attached to each of its four corners. The rings on the upper corners were fastened by a gold chain to the shoulderpieces of the ephod. The lower rings were fastened just above the curious girdle with blue laces to the two gold rings on the ephod. The breastplate was over the heart of Aaron as a reminder of his responsibility for making decisions on behalf of the nation (Exod. 28:29–30).

The robe of the ephod was blue and probably hung to the feet. The hole for the head was a simple circle woven around its edge to prevent tearing. Along its bottom hem were blue, purple, and

Shoulder pieces

scarlet pomegranate shaped ornaments, alternately attached with gold bells. How many bells and pomegranate ornaments used is not known. The importance attached to wearing the robe of the ephod is stated in Exodus 28:35: "And it shall be upon Aaron to minister: and his sound shall be heard when he goeth in unto the holy place before the Lord, and when he cometh out, that he die not." Thus, the tinkling of the bells was to be a solemn reminder to Aaron that he was approaching God to minister on behalf of the nation.

The mitre was the special headdress reserved solely for the high priest (Exod. 28:36–38; 39:30, 31). It was made of white linen and was probably turban shaped. Its only ornament was a gold plate and a blue ribbon used to fasten the plate to the mitre. The most

Levitical Priesthood

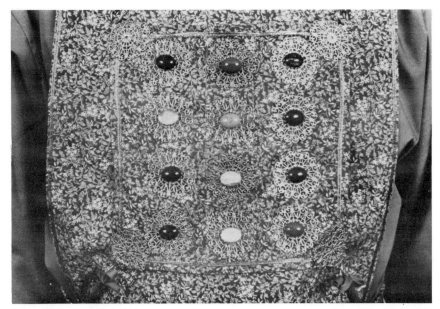

Breastplate

Ephod with pomegranate ornaments and bells

Mitre with gold plate

significant thing about the mitre was the inscription on the plate, which read, "Holiness to the Lord." This signified the consecration of the high priest, whose work as a mediator, through the offering of sacrifices, typified the efficacy of Christ as our high priest and as the "Lamb of God" who takes away the sins of the world.

The broidered coat of fine linen was worn under the robe of the ephod, and probably reached to the feet (Exod. 28:39; 39:27). It is not clear whether or not it showed beneath the robe of the ephod. The Hebrew word for *broider,* used in Exodus 28:4 and embroider used in Exodus 28:39, implies some special method of weaving, not needlework. From Leviticus 8:7 we learn that the broidered coat, like the ephod, had a girdle or sash of its own.

Garments for the sons of Aaron are listed in Exodus 28:40–41. They consisted of only a coat and girdle. Their headdress, called a bonnet, was probably similar to the high priest's mitre, although smaller. Both high priest and priests were instructed to wear linen breeches or undergarments (Exod. 28:42–43). The punishment for not wearing them was death. This is in contrast to heathen priests who often ministered naked.

Levitical Priesthood

Anointing

Aaron's anointing of consecration, in which he was anointed with oil and which served as a ceremonial means of consecrating a person or object to the work of the Lord, followed immediately after he was initially dressed in his priestly clothing (Exod. 29:7, 40:13 and Lev. 8:12). The method of anointing Aaron was performed differently than that of his sons. Oil was poured upon

Moses anoints Aaron with oil

Aaron's head as described in Psalm 133:2, and the oil was said to run down upon his beard and his garments. Only Aaron and each of the subsequent high priests were anointed in this manner (Exod. 29:29–30, Lev. 16:32 and 21:10). Because of this practice, the high priest is referred to as the priest that is anointed (Lev. 4:5, 16, 6:22 and Num. 35:25). Likewise, Jesus is called the Messiah (John 1:41) or anointed one.

Exodus 40:15 state that the sons of Aaron were to be anointed as their father. This is not a reference to the same kind of initial anointing Aaron received, but to an additional anointing of Aaron and his sons that took place after the completion of their consecration and special offerings. At this time, oil and blood were sprinkled upon them, establishing them as an everlasting priesthood. (Exod. 28:41; 29:21; 30:30; Lev. 8:30). It was not to be repeated, as was the special anointing of each new high priest. The oil and blood used in their sanctification represented the anointing oil of the Lord that would endue them with power for their work and cleanse them from sin (blood).

Offerings

Offerings were made after the special anointing of Aaron and before the second anointing of both Aaron and his sons (Exod. 29:10–29; Lev. 8:14–29). Both Aaron and his sons were treated as equals in regard to the offerings because they all needed atonement for their sin, unlike Jesus, our true high priest, who could say, "the prince of this world cometh, and hath nothing in me (John 14:30)." The offering was a bullock, which is the prescribed sin offering for the high priest (Lev. 4:3) There is, however, a deviation here from the usual instructions related to the sin offering for the high priest. The blood of the sin offering for the high priest was normally taken into the sanctuary (Lev. 4:5–7), and the flesh eaten by the priests (Lev. 6:26). In this instance, neither was done. This can be explained by the fact that Moses was acting in the priestly capacity since Aaron and his sons were not yet officially priests.

Following the sin offering, a ram was sacrificed as a burnt offering, which was sacrificed according to established procedures. The last offering of their consecration was a special peace or thanksgiving offering (Lev. 3; 7:11–15). The sacrificial ram was called the ram of consecration or filling because parts of it were placed in the palms of Aaron and his sons to be waved before the Lord as a wave offering; thus the filling of their hands was one of the means used to effect their consecration. The wave offering always signified gifts offered to God's service.

The most peculiar aspect of the ram of consecration was the special application of its blood, which was applied to the right ear, right thumb and right big toe of Aaron and his sons. The application of blood to the ear signified that they were to hear and obey God's laws; its application to the thumb signified the use of their hands for priestly work and the application to the toe signified they were always to walk in his ways.

These rituals and offerings we have just described were repeated daily during the next six days to complete their consecration. During this period, they remained in the court of the tabernacle (Exod. 29:35; Lev. 8:33–35).

Upon the completion of the priest's consecration, the dedication of the brazen altar, which was being dedicated concurrently with the priests, continued another five days. The consecration of the tribe of Levi followed (Num. 8:5–14; 20–22). The consecration of the Levites was performed differently than the priests' consecration. It lasted one day. There was no ceremonial washing, clothing with special garments, anointing with holy oil, sprinkling with blood, or special sacrifices. Nevertheless, it was a solemn and impressive consecration which consisted of three parts: purification, presentation, and sacrifice.

The Levites' purification included the ceremonial sprinkling with the water of purifying, from an unexplained source, which typified their cleansing from sin. Furthermore, the purification process included the shaving of all their body hair and the washing of their clothing. The reason for sprinkling instead of washing may have been due to their number (22,000, or 8,580 if only those of the age qualified to minister were consecrated), but if this and the following acts were done by representation with only a few of the Levites, there seems to be no adequate reason for just sprinkling. Some believe that the water of purifying was prepared in the same manner as the water of separation mentioned in Numbers 19, but this seems unlikely. Instructions for the water of separation were not given until after the Israelites' arrival at Kadesh-barnea.

There were two distinct acts in the presentation of the Levites.

The first was the transference of the work of the priesthood from the entire congregation to the Levites. This was done by the laying on of hands and possibly by a representation of only a few Levites. The second act, which is closely related to the first, was Aaron's offer of the Levites as a wave offering to the Lord. The Hebrew words *offer* in Numbers 8:11 and *offered* in 8:21 are best translated as wave. The Lord had chosen the Levites instead of the firstborn, so the waving acknowledged that they were his and would be used in his service at the tabernacle. Just as other wave offerings were given to the priests, so were the Levites (Num. 3:9). How the waving of the Levites was accomplished is not explained, but since they could not have been literally waved, it must have been performed symbolically.

A sin offering and burnt offering were both offered at this time to make atonement for the sin of the Levites.

Their Work

In their reconciliatory ministry, the work of the priests and the Levites entailed many different duties. Aaron and his sons constituted the priest office (Num. 3:3), whereas the Levites were ministers unto the priests as well as at the tabernacle (Num. 3:6). The work of the high priest was that of general overseer of the tabernacle and all that pertained to it. The other priests were his assistants and, as such, they performed all priestly duties except the rituals on the Day of Atonement, sin offering for himself and the congregation, which were the exclusive duties of the high priest.

The following is a list of the tasks the priests performed: performing all offerings and sacrifices (Lev. 1–7), which included all daily, weekly, monthly, and yearly sacrifices; preserving the fire on the brazen altar (Lev. 6:13); keeping the lamp burning (Exod. 27:20); burning incense (Exod. 30:7–8); providing shewbread (Lev. 24:8); covering the furniture before the camp is moved (Num. 4:15); diagnosing diseases of the nation (Lev. 13–15); administering the law of jealousy (Num. 5); administering the Nazarite vow (Num. 6:13–21); blowing of the trumpets (Num. 10:1–10; pronouncing benediction (Num. 6:24–27); teaching the law (Lev. 10:11, Deut. 24:8; 31:9–13 and Deut. 33:10); compounding the holy anointing oil and sweet incense (Exod. 30:22–28); purifying the

Levitical Priesthood   89

ceremonially unclean (Lev. 15:31); preparing the water of separation (Num. 19); ascertaining the value of devoted things to be redeemed (Lev. 27:8–12); encouraging the army before battle (Deut. 20:2–4); inquiring of God for the nation (Exod. 28:30); and working within the judicial system to ensure that justice would be according to God's laws (Deut. 17:8–13; 19:17; 21:1–9).

It is readily apparent that the priests had enormous responsibilities concerning national, civil and moral matters, which made the priests' office the most important office in the nation. Not until the nation's rule by kings would there be an office that would rival the priesthood in importance and power. Even then, when the king wanted to inquire of the Lord in matters of national importance, he would go to the high priest, who used the urim and thummim (1 Sam. 23:9–12; 28:6). The consequences of not seeking God's counsel can be seen in the deception the Gibeonites perpetrated on Israel (Josh. 9:14).

The task of taking down and setting up of the tabernacle was not the work of the priests, but belonged solely to the three sons of Levi: the Kohathites, the Gershonites and the Merarites. This

Levites erect the tabernacle

was their principal work; "But thou shalt appoint the Levites over the tabernacle of testimony, and over all the vessels thereof, and over all things that belong to it: they shall bear the tabernacle, and all the vessels thereof; and they shall minister unto it, and shall encamp round about the tabernacle. And when the tabernacle setteth forward, the Levites shall take it down: and when the tabernacle is to be pitched, the Levites shall set it up: and the stranger that cometh nigh shall be put to death" (Num. 1:50, 51). The Levites camped around the tabernacle to be close to their work and to act as guards against unlawful approach (Num. 1:53). The priests camped before the tabernacle, on the east side, for the same reason (Num. 3:38).

The assembling and disassembling of the tabernacle was accomplished quite rapidly. Given the three sons of Levi, who each had specific duties to perform when the tabernacle was moved and the special design of the tabernacle, it was possible to set it up or take it down in a matter of a few hours (Num. 10:21). There was ample manpower for the work. At the time of the first numbering of the Levites, there were 8,580 who met the age requirements for service, more than enough to do the work at the tabernacle (Num. 4:47–48). Numbers 8:24 says they were to "wait" upon the service of the tabernacle. The word *wait* is also translated "mustered" (2 Kings 25:19 and Jer. 52:25). This implies the Levites were to be ready to be called to service because, naturally, all of them could not serve at the same time.

The following are the specific duties of each of the three sons of Levi:

The chief Kohathite was Elizathan (Num. 3:30). His family was located south of the tabernacle (Num. 3:29). They were responsible for carrying the holy furniture of the tabernacle on their shoulders (Num. 7:9). This included the ark, the table of shewbread, the candlestick, the incense altar, and the brazen altar. Although the laver is not mentioned, it was certainly carried by the Kohathites. They were also responsible for the vessels used with the furniture (Num. 3:31 and 4:4–15).

Eleazar, Aaron's son, had specific oversight of the Kohathites and the tabernacle (Num. 3:32; 4:16). Since he was in line to be the next high priest, this may indicate that the next priest to succeed as high priest would always inherit this particular duty—charge of the oil for the candlestick, the sweet incense, the daily meat offering, the anointing oil, and the vessels of the sanctuary (Num. 4:16).

Although the Kohathites were to carry the holy furniture, they were forbidden to touch (Num. 4:15) or even see (Num. 4:20) the furniture before the priests had covered them (Num. 4:5–15) and appointed the Kohathites who were to carry them (Num. 4:19). The penalty for not heeding these instructions was death (Num. 4:15; 20). This may seem a severe punishment, but God required reverence for his instructions as exemplified when David sought to bring the ark from the house of Abinadab to Jerusalem. David failed to heed these instructions and Uzzah was struck dead when he touched the ark to steady it (2 Sam. 6:6–7). This death had the good effect of causing David to search the scripture he had neglected (1 Chron. 15:2, 12–14).

The Gershonites were camped west of the tabernacle (Num. 3:23). Their chief was Eliasaph (Num. 3:24). Ithamar, Aaron's son, had charge over the Gershonites (Num. 4:28). They were to carry the four coverings of the tabernacle; the outer veil, the curtain of the outer court and its gate, and the cords and instruments used in their work (Num. 3:25; 4:24–28). The inner veil is not mentioned because it was the first covering of the ark.

The twelve princes of Israel gave an offering of six wagons and twelve oxen which were distributed to the three sons of Levi according to their need at the time of the dedication of the altar. The Kohathites did not receive any wagons or oxen because they carried the furniture of the tabernacle on their shoulders (Num. 7:9). Two wagons and four oxen were given to the Gershonites. The remaining four wagons and eight oxen were given to the Merarites.

The Merarites pitched their tents on the north side of the tabernacle. Their chief was Zuriel (Num. 3:35). They were responsible for the boards, bars, sockets, and pillars of the sanctuary, as well as the pillars, sockets, pins and cords of the outer court and the instruments needed for their work (Num. 3:36, 37; 4:31, 32). These metallic parts of the tabernacle weighed more than nine tons, so the Merarites easily had the greatest burden. Thus, they received the largest number of wagons and oxen (four wagons, eight oxen) from the offerings of the princes of Israel (Num. 7:2–3). Ithamar also had the charge over the Merarites (Num. 4:33).

One duty the Levites no longer had to perform after their arrival in the Promised Land was supplying the tabernacle with wood and water. This was supplied by the Gibeonites, their punishment for deceiving the nation (Josh. 9:27).

Although these were the initial duties of the Levites, with the arrival of the tabernacle at a more permanent location in the Promised Land and the later building of the temple, many of these duties became unnecessary. "For David said, The Lord God of Israel hath given rest unto his people, that they may dwell in Jerusalem for ever: and also unto the Levites; they shall no more carry the tabernacle, nor any vessels of it for the service thereof" (1 Chron. 23:25–26). So, at the beginning of Solomon's reign and under the guidance of David (1 Chron. 23:6), the duties of the Levites were changed (1 Chron. 23:4–6; 26–28).

Immediately prior to this time, the Levites were numbered from the ages of thirty upward. They totalled 38,000 (1 Chron. 23:3). Although the span of thirty to fifty years of age was the first established ages for their census (Num. 4:3), it was soon lowered to twenty-five (Num. 8:24–25). Why they were again numbered from thirty and upward at the beginning of Solomon's reign is not known. Later, during Solomon's reign, the age was lowered to twenty and above (1 Chron. 23:27). The lower age was needed to assure that there were enough Levites to perform their new duties, since they were no longer to carry the tabernacle.

Of the 38,000 Levites numbered, 24,000 were to be workers, 6,000 officers and judges, 4,000 porters and 4,000 musicians. To facilitate their work, they were divided into twenty-four courses of one-week duty (1 Chron. 23–26). These new instructions for their duties and courses of the Levites were given to David by the Spirit of God (1 Chron. 24:19; 28:11–13), and not arbitrarily established by him.

It is evident that the priests and the Levites had to work together as a well-drilled team in their work at the tabernacle. A demonstration of this is illustrated when they moved the tabernacle with each relocation of their camp. The signal to the nation that a journey to another location was to begin was the movement of the cloud from over the tabernacle (Exod. 40:36–37). With this signal the whole nation went into action (see chart on page 97).

The priest and Levites alone prepared for the movement of the tabernacle. Aaron and Eleazar went first into the sanctuary to cover the holy furniture with their respective coverings (see chart page 98). Each piece had to be covered before the Kohathites could carry it. The first item to be covered was the ark (Num. 4:5). To accomplish this the priests used long poles to unhook the inner veil, then walked forward to cover the ark. Thus, no one ever saw the ark, except the high priest and then only once a year on the Day of Atonement. The priests then covered the other items. Eleazar was responsible for making sure that the anointing oil, sweet incense, and daily meat offerings were properly secured for the journey (Num. 4:16). When these things were accomplished, the appointment of the individual Kohathites to carry the furnishings was made. While these duties were being performed in the sanctuary, Ithamar, who had charge of the Gershonites and Merarites, was seeing to the disassembling of the outer court.

As soon as the furnishings were covered, the work of disassembling the sanctuary structure began. The Gershonites began by removing the coverings as the Merarites disassembled the walls and pillars. The heavier parts were loaded into the wagons while the rest was carried by other vehicles or bodily. As stated earlier, considering the special design of the tabernacle and the organization of the priests and Levites, it was probably a matter of only a few hours before the tabernacle was ready for travel.

When all was ready, both the tabernacle and the nation, Eleazar and Ithamar would blow an alarm of short, sharp tones on silver trumpets (Num. 10:1–6). This was the signal for the three tribes located east of the tabernacle (Judah, Issachar, and Zebulun) to go forward. They were followed by the Gershonites and Merarites who transported the tabernacle (Num. 10:14–17). A second alarm by the priests signaled the tribes on the south (Gad, Simeon, and Reuben) to journey. The Kohathites followed the tribes on the south with the ark and other items of the sanctuary. This placed them in the center of the march (Num. 10:18–21). The third alarm signaled the tribes on the west (Ephraim, Manasseh and Benjamin) to journey. The fourth alarm signaled the tribes on the north (Dan, Asher, Naphtali) (Num. 10:22–28).

The Israelites would then follow the guiding presence of the cloud. When the cloud tarried, the three leading tribes would stop and camp facing east. This put the Gershonites and Merarites in their proper position for setting up the tabernacle. Numbers 10:21 implies they could have at least the walls, pillars and outer veil set up before the Kohathites arrived with the furnishings. The other tribes, on their arrival, would then set their tents in their proper position about the tabernacle.

The Levites were amply recompensed for their work at the tabernacle. Their primary source of income was from the tithes of the nation: "And, behold, I have given the children of Levi all the tenth in Israel for an inheritance, for their service which they serve, even the service of the tabernacle of the congregation" (Num. 18:21). Unlike the other tribes, the Levites did not inherit any specific area of land but were scattered over the whole of the Promised Land, thus fulfilling Genesis 49:7. "And the Lord spake unto Aaron, Thou shalt have no inheritance in their land, neither shalt thou have any part among them: I am thy part and thine inheritance" (Num. 18:20). These things they inherited in the sense that things dedicated to God were used for their support. Nevertheless, the Levites were given forty-eight cities and fields for the pasture of their cattle. With the tithes and cities, the Levites were well-supported.

The support of the priests was from a wider variety of sources. One source was the tithes from the Levites (Num. 18:28). Another was the specific portions of the sacrifices that were not burned on the altar (Num. 18:9–10). All of these were to be eaten in the outer court by only the priests. This included the meat offering (Lev. 6:16), sin offering (Lev. 6:26), trespass offering (Lev. 7:6), and the shewbread (Lev. 24:9). They are called "the most holy" because they were eaten in the outer court. The only exception to this rule was the heave and wave offerings of the peace offering. (Exod. 29:26–28; Lev. 7:31–36), which could be eaten only by the priests' family as long as they were clean (Num. 8:11). The other sources of support came from fines (Lev. 5:6), spoils of war (Num. 31:26–29; Lev. 10:14), devoted things (Num. 5:10, 18:14; Lev. 27), redemption money (Exod. 13:13; Num. 3:46–51; Num. 18:15–16), thirteen cities in Judah, Simeon, and Benjamin (Josh. 21:4–5), firstborn (Num. 3:51; 18:15), and first fruits (Deut. 18:3–5; Num. 18:12–13). This same principle of support is taught in the New Testament concerning support of the ministry (1 Cor. 9:13–14).

It is obvious that these means of support brought in a vast amount of revenue for the Levites and priests, but these methods were effective only as long as the people were totally surrendered to God by following his laws and precepts (Neh. 13:10–13 and Deut. 12:28).

Levitical Priesthood 95

Four Generations

This chart shows graphically how all priests could be Levites and why all Levites were not priests. It can also be used to explain the four generations of Genesis 15:16 (see history).

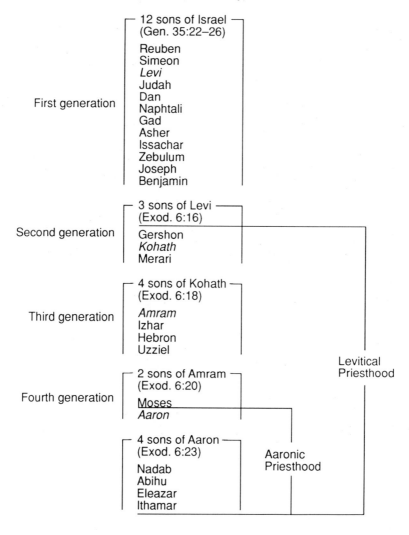

The High Priest

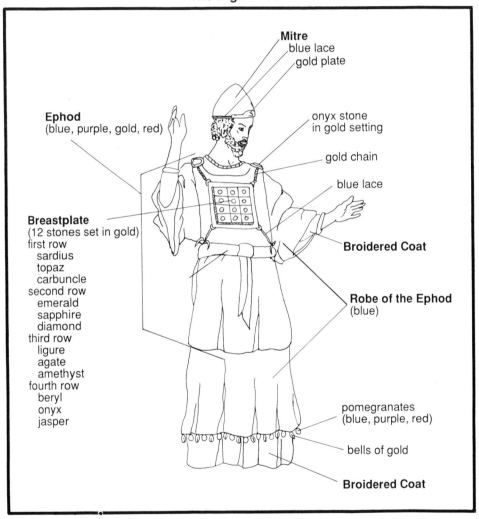

Placement of Tabernacle

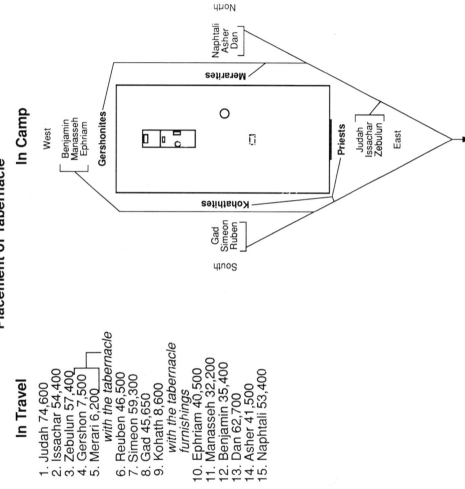

In Camp

West: Benjamin, Manasseh, Ephraim — Gershonites
North: Naphtali, Asher, Dan — Merarites
East: Judah, Issachar, Zebulun — Priests
South: Gad, Simeon, Ruben — Kohathites

In Travel

1. Judah 74,600
2. Issachar 54,400
3. Zebulun 57,400
4. Gershon 7,500
5. Merari 6,200
   with the tabernacle
6. Reuben 46,500
7. Simeon 59,300
8. Gad 45,650
9. Kohath 8,600
   with the tabernacle furnishings
10. Ephriam 40,500
11. Manasseh 32,200
12. Benjamin 35,400
13. Dan 62,700
14. Asher 41,500
15. Naphtali 53,400

Table 4 **Coverings for the Furnishings During Travel Numbers 4:4–15**

Furnishings	First covering	Second covering	Third covering
Ark	veil (inner)	badger's skin	blue cloth
table of shewbread	blue cloth	scarlet cloth	badger's skin
candlestick	blue cloth	badger's skin	none
golden altar	blue cloth	badger's skin	none
other instruments of ministry	blue cloth	badger's skin	none
brazen altar	purple cloth	badger's skin	none
laver	none is given	none is given	none is given

5 The Typology of the Tabernacle

"Who serve unto the example and shadow of heavenly things" (Heb. 8:5).

Shadows of heavenly things

Without a doubt, the tabernacle is the most written about type in Scripture. More than forty-five chapters are devoted to the tabernacle and the activities that took place there. No other type is so thoroughly dealt with. In response to its obvious importance, Christians have written profusely about it, probably more so than any other type. Among the writings, one will discover a variety of themes and interpretations. There are several reasons for this variety, but a popular one is extremism.

The extremist is one who finds types everywhere in Scripture and makes every detail of them significant, finding unlimited meaning to every jot and tittle. Their only guidelines for defining a type seem to be general notions and indefinite ideals. Because they do not discipline their imaginations, they arrive at widely different and speculative conclusions. They usually emphasize the colors, materials, and even the numbers of some objects of the tabernacle, without a plain scripture reference to support their conclusions. No one would use this method in understanding any other book; why do so with the Bible, especially since the Bible is its own commentator?

If one wants to understand types correctly, one should follow wise guidelines. Extremists often over-spiritualize the Word of God to such an extent that they distort its true and plain meaning. One needs to read and interpret the Bible as any other book.

Every type is confirmed in scripture as a type. This is the first principle in understanding types, that blue is held to typify heaven; purple, royalty; silver, redemption; brass, judgment; twelve, administration; the four pillars of the tabernacle, the four Gospels, and so on, may be generally held true, but where can one find a scriptural passage to prove it?

When we seek to understand a type, we need to have a clear and concise definition of a type. Well-defined borders are necessary to keep one from straying from intended meanings, because nothing more than the Bible's intended meaning should be stressed. If similar guidelines were followed by all Bible students, their conclusions would certainly be much closer. The extremist's approach often implies that there are mysterious meanings to every detail of scripture, destroying the simplicity of God's word.

Another reason for the variety of interpretations concerning the tabernacle has to do with one's knowledge. To properly understand any type, and this is especially true of the tabernacle because of the amount of scripture concerning it, one must have a good knowledge of both the Old and New Testament. This is true because a fundamental element of all types is their corresponding relationship in the Old and New Testament.

One can easily determine that the account of the construction of the tabernacle in Exodus reveals God's detailed planning. Moses was told to "see that thou make it according to the pattern" (Heb. 8:5), and he was careful, examining each step of its construction to make sure it was built according to that pattern (Exod. 39:43). Should we be any less particular in our study of the tabernacle?

The Typology of the Tabernacle

In the following pages, I will define a type, set boundaries for interpretation and categorize the types found in the tabernacle.

Definition: A type is a preordained person, event or object of the Old Testament that prefigures a corresponding person, event, or object in the New Testament in such a way that their common characteristics establish them as an identifiable class. There are several Greek words that express this definition:

1. *Tupos:* translated as figure (Rom. 5:14), pattern (Heb. 8:5), ensample (1 Cor. 10:11) and as example (1 Cor. 10:6).
2. *Anti-tupon:* translated as like figure (1 Peter 3:21), and as figure (Heb. 9:24).
3. *Hupodeigma:* translated as pattern (Heb. 9:23), ensample (2 Peter 2:6) and example (Heb. 4:11).
4. *Parabole:* translated as figure (Heb. 9:9; 11:19).
5. *Skia:* translated as shadow (Col. 2:17; Heb. 8:5; 10:1).

Although the writers of the New Testament used various words to express a type, each word always expressed the idea of some likeness between two persons, events, or objects. The Greek word *skia,* translated "shadow," corresponds best to our English word *type,* because like a shadow, it expresses the reality it foreshadows.

The two essential elements of a type can be illustrated by a shadow and the object which casts the shadow. The reality is always in the object and not in the shadow. If you see only the shadow, your understanding of the reality, or the object, will be limited. This is why the Old Testament saints had only a limited degree of understanding of certain New Testament truths and events. "For verily I say unto you, That many prophets and righteous men have desired to see those things which ye see, and have not seen them; and to hear those things which ye hear, and have not heard them" (Matt. 13:17). How much greater our understanding should be. We see the reality of what they saw only in shadow. The popular saying, "the New Testament is in the old concealed and the old is in the new revealed," is demonstrated best in types, and especially the types of the tabernacle.

In typology these two elements, the shadow and the object, are called the type and the antitype, respectively. The type (shadow) is always found in the Old Testament and is the preordained shadow of the antitype (object). The antitype is found in the New

Testament and is the reality, or fulfillment, of what the type prefigured.

Three basic rules are necessary for the proper interpretation of types:

1. Each type will have one central truth to which the whole type will agree. This truth will always harmonize with the rest of Scripture, and only this intended truth should be emphasized.
2. The only authority for a type is the Bible. Types cannot be created because of some similarity between two things in scripture. There must always be scripture to confirm every type because both the type and the antitype are preordained of God. Only as much of the Old Testament is to be considered typical as the New Testament confirms. An example of this is the life of Joseph compared to that of Christ. There are many similarities between them, but because there is no corresponding relationship between them in scripture, the life of Joseph cannot be considered a biblical type.
3. Types should be understood and interpreted only in light of their antitype. Although there may be many other things in the type that the antitype does not speak of (as in the type of the tabernacle), only the points of resemblance between the type and antitype should be emphasized. Ignoring this rule often leads to the erroneous idea that every peg, cord, pillar, covering, of the tabernacle is of some significance.

Table 5 is a list of true biblical types which are treated in this book. A few common analogies are also included.

The following is a short explanation of the types in the tabernacle and other related types along with their scriptural foundation.

Type: Old Testament tabernacle

(Exod. 25–31; 35–40)

Antitype: True tabernacle or gospel program

Hebrews 8:1–2: Now of the things which we have spoken this is the sum: We have such an high priest, who is set on the right

Table 5 **Types of Antitypes**

Type	Antitype
tabernacle	gospel
sanctuary (holy place and holy of holies)	Heaven
outer court*	earth
furniture of tabernacle	ministries of Christ
brazen altar	Calvary
laver	Christ's sinlessness
candlestick	ministry of imparting the Holy Spirit
table of shewbread	sustaining power of Christ for the believer
incense altar	Christ's ministry of intercession
holy of holies	presence of God
ark	God, attribute of justice
mercy seat	God, attribute of mercy
veil	flesh of Christ
high priest	Christ
other priests	no significance, merely assistants to the high priest
Levites*	ministers of the Gospel. They came out of Israel (Church) and their duty was to carry the tabernacle (Gospel).
physical perfection of priests and sacrificial animals	Christ's sinlessness
blood	efficacy of Christ's life and sacrificial death
sin offering for the high priest and congregation	Christ's death outside the gates of Jerusalem
Day of Atonement	efficacy of Christ's one sacrifice for the sins of the world
animal sacrifices	Christ's sacrificial death life and death
burnt offering	consecration of Christ to God, consecration of saints to God
meat offering	service of Christ to man; service of man to his fellowman
sin and trespass offerings	Christ's provision of atonement; man's appropriation
peace offering	result of Christ's expiatory death; a means for man to express reconciliation and communication
Egypt*	the world and the bondage it brings
Canaan*	the world in which the believer has freedom and victory in God
Israel*	the church, God's people
Wilderness*	the backslidden believer

*Analogies drawn from their relationship to the type.

hand of the throne of the Majesty in the heavens; A minister of the sanctuary, and of the true tabernacle, which the Lord pitched, and not man.

Hebrews 9:1–11: Then verily the first covenant had also ordinances of divine service, and a worldly sanctuary. For there was a tabernacle made; the first, wherein was the candlestick, and the table, and the shewbread; which is called the Holiest of all: Which had the golden censer, and the ark of the covenant overlaid round about with gold, wherein was the golden pot that had manna, and Aaron's rod that budded, and the tables of the covenant; And over it the cherubims of glory shadowing the mercyseat; of which we cannot now speak particularly. Now when these things were thus ordained, the priests went always in the first tabernacle, accomplishing the service of God. But into the second went the high priest alone once every year, not without blood, which he offered for himself, and for the errors of the people: The Holy Ghost this signifying, that the way into the holiest of all was not yet made manifest, while as the first tabernacle was yet standing: Which was a figure for the time then present, in which were offered both gifts and sacrifices, that could not make him that did the service perfect, as pertaining to the conscience; Which stood only in meats and drinks, and divers washings, and carnal ordinances, imposed on them until the time of reformation. But Christ being come an high priest of good things to come, by a greater and more perfect tabernacle, not made with hands, that is to say, not of this building.

Hebrews 9:24: For Christ is not entered into the holy places made with hands, which are the figures of the true; but into heaven itself, now to appear in the presence of God for us:

It is obvious from these scriptural passages that the tabernacle and many things associated with it: the priesthood (Heb. 8:1), sacrifices (Heb. 8:3–5), furnishings (Heb. 9:1–9), and ordinances (Heb. 9:10), were typical of the true tabernacle (Heb. 8:2). But what is the true tabernacle? As you become more familiar with the other tabernacle types and see how they relate to one another, you will see they can only refer to the gospel.

The greater and more perfect (complete) tabernacle of Hebrews 9:11 refers to the true tabernacle, or gospel, which is now complete because Christ has died for the sins of man, completing the work of redemption (Heb. 9:12). The incompleteness of the Old Testament tabernacle established it as a type to foreshadow the gospel plan. It was completed (Heb. 9:8, 9) when Christ came to die for the sins of the world. Thus, Old Testament saints had the gospel preached to them through the type of the tabernacle: "For unto us was the gospel preached, as well as unto them" (Heb. 4:2).

Type: High Priest

Exodus 28:1: And take thou unto thee Aaron thy brother, and his sons with him, from among the children of Israel, that he may minister unto me the priest's office, even Aaron, Nadab and Abihu, Eleazar and Ithamar, Aaron's sons.

Antitype: Christ

Hebrews 4:14–15: Seeing then that we have a great high priest, that is passed into the heavens, Jesus the Son of God, let us hold fast our profession. For we have not an high priest which cannot be touched with the feeling of our infirmities; but was in all points tempted like as we are, yet without sin.

Hebrews 5:1–5: For every high priest taken from among men is ordained for men in things pertaining to God, that he may offer both gifts and sacrifices for sins: Who can have compassion on the ignorant, and on them that are out of the way; for that he himself also is compassed with infirmity. And by reason thereof he ought, as for the people, so also for himself, but that he is called of God, as was Aaron. So also Christ glorified not himself to be made an high priest; but that he said unto him, Thou art my Son, to day have I begotten thee.

Hebrews 7:24–28: But this man, because he continueth ever, hath an unchangeable priesthood. Wherefore he is able to save them to the uttermost that come unto God by him, seeing he ever liveth to make intercession for them. For such an high priest became us, who is holy, harmless, undefiled; separate from sinners, and made higher than the heavens: Who needeth not daily, as those high priests, to offer up sacrifice, first for his own sins, and then for the people's: for this he did once, when he offered up himself. For the law maketh men high priests which have infirmity; but the word of oath, which was since the law, maketh the Son, who is consecrated for evermore.

Hebrews 8:1–6: Now of the things which we have spoken this is the sum: We have such an high priest, who is set on the right hand of the throne of the Majesty in the heavens; A minister of the sanctuary, and of the true tabernacle, which the Lord pitched, and not man. For every high priest is ordained to offer gifts and sacrifices; wherefore it is of necessity that this man have somewhat also to offer. For if he were on earth, he should not be a priest, seeing that there are priests that offer gifts accordingly to the law: Who serve unto the example and shadow of heavenly things, as Moses was admonished of God when he was about to make the tabernacle: for, See, saith he, that thou make all things according to the pattern shewed to thee in the mount. But now hath he obtained a more excellent ministry, by how much also he is the mediator of a better covenant, which was established upon better promises.

Hebrews 9:11: But Christ being come an high priest of good things to come, by a greater and more perfect tabernacle, not made with hands, that is to say, not of this building.

Hebrews 9:24–25: For Christ is not entered into the holy places made with hands, which are the figures of the true; but into heaven itself, now to appear in the presence of God for us: Nor yet that he should offer himself often, as the high priest entereth into the holy place every year with blood of others.

There are many scriptures in the New Testament that confirm the high priest of the tabernacle as a type of Christ.

One of the functions of the high priest was to offer sacrifices, which typified Christ's offering of himself. The high priest, not able to be both priest and the offering, offered the animal to typify Christ, who is our high priest as well as our offering (Heb. 8:3–4; 10:5).

Very often priests, Aaron's sons, are considered to be a type of the Christian. There is no scriptural basis for this in the antitype sense. However, Peter does make reference to Christians as priests in 1 Peter 2:5, and John in Revelation 5:10. Old Testament priests were only assistants to the high priest because he was not able to do all the work himself. He was subject to death and would need someone to take his place when he died. Hebrews 7:23: "And they truly were many priests, because they were not suffered to continue by reason of death." For them to represent Christians would destroy the basic type of the tabernacle as the Gospel. We should understand our priesthood as similar to that of the Levites (see page 88).

Type: Furniture of the tabernacle
Exodus 25:10–40; 27:1–8; 30:1–10, 17–21)

Antitype: Ministries of Christ

Hebrews 8:2: A minister of the sanctuary, and of the true tabernacle, which the Lord pitched, and not man.

Hebrews 9:1–5: Then verily the first covenant had also ordinances of divine service, and a worldly sanctuary. For there was a tabernacle made; the first, wherein, was the candlestick, and the table, and the shewbread; which is called the sanctuary. And after the second veil, the tabernacle which is called the Holiest of all; Which had the golden censer, and the ark of the covenant overlaid round about with gold, wherein was the golden pot that had manna, and Aaron's rod that budded, and the tables of the covenant; And over it the cherubims of glory shadowing the mercyseat; of which we cannot now speak particularly.

Usually the various furnishings are considered types of Christ in themselves, but they should be understood as representing various ministries of Christ. Individually they do not represent types of Christ anymore than they represent types of priests. They do, however, clearly represent the different aspects of his ministry as they also did for the high priest (Heb. 8:2 and 10:11). Nowhere in Scripture do we find anything that would indicate that the furnishings were individual types of Christ or that they represented various ministries of the Church or Christians as they are often taught to do. To make them such would destroy the purpose of the tabernacle as representing the gospel. (For an explanation of each item, see chapters 6 and 7).

Type: Holy place and holy of holies (sanctuary)

Antitype: Heaven

Hebrews 9:23–24: It was therefore necessary that the patterns of things in the heavens should be purified with these; but the heavenly things themselves with better sacrifices than these. For Christ is not entered into the holy places made with hands, which are the figures of the true; but into heaven itself, now to appear in the presence of God for us;

The word "places" refers to the two compartments of the sanctuary, the holy place and the holy of holies, as representatives of heaven. We can, therefore, identify the furniture of the holy place as heavenly ministries of Christ. The brazen altar would then be an earthly ministry being in the outer court. Just as the high priest, a minister of the worldly sanctuary, ministered at the candlestick, the table of shewbread and incense altar (Heb. 9:1–2), so Christ is in heaven ministering on our behalf in the presence of God. The language of verse 9:23 is to be taken figuratively and not literally, simply because there is no literal tabernacle in heaven (Heb. 8:5) in which Christ serves as the high priest did on earth. These patterns in heaven are the reality of what the tabernacle could only imperfectly represent on earth, even though a golden incense altar and the ark are in heaven (Rev. 8:3; 9:13; 11:19).

Type: Ark and mercyseat

Antitype: God

Hebrews 9:24: For Christ is not entered into the holy places made with hands, which are the figures of the true; but into heaven itself, now to appear in the presence of God for us (For explanation, see chapter 8).

Type: Animal sacrifices

(Leviticus 1–7)

Antitype: Christ's sacrificial life and death

John 1:29: The next day John seeth Jesus coming unto him, and saith, Behold the Lamb of God, which taketh away the sin of the world.

1 Corinthians 5:7: For even Christ our passover is sacrificed for us.

Ephesians 5:2: And walk in love, as Christ also hath loved us, and hath given himself for us an offering and a sacrifice to God for a sweetsmelling savour.

Hebrews 9:28: So Christ was once offered to bear the sins of many; and unto them that look for him shall he appear the second time without sin unto salvation.

Hebrews 10:1–2: For the law having a shadow of good things to come, and not the very image of the things, can never with those sacrifices which they offered year by year continually make the comers thereunto perfect. For then would they not have ceased to be offered? because that the worshippers once purged have had no more conscience of sins. But in those sacrifices there is a remembrance again made of sins every year. For it is not possible that the blood of bulls and goats should take away sins. Wherefore when he cometh into the world, he saith, Sacrifice and offering thou wouldest not, but a body hast thou prepared me: In burnt offerings and sacrifices for sin thou hast had no pleasure. Then said I, Lo, I come (in the volume of the book it is written of me,) to do thy will, O God. Above when he said, Sacrifice and offering and burnt offerings and offering for sin thou wouldest not, neither hadst pleasure therein;

which are offered by the law: Then said he, Lo, I come to do thy will, O God. He taketh away the first, that he may establish the second. By the which will we are sanctified through the offering of the body of Jesus Christ once for all. And every priest standeth daily ministering and offering oftentimes the same sacrifices, which can never take away sins: But this man, after he had offered one sacrifice for sins for ever, sat down on the right hand of God;

1 Peter 1:18–19: Forasmuch as ye know that ye were not redeemed with corruptible things, as silver and gold, from your vain conversation received by tradition from your fathers; But with the precious blood of Christ, as of a lamb without blemish and without spot.

Revelation 5:9: And they sung a new song, saying, Thou art worthy to take the book, and to open the seals thereof: for thou wast slain, and hast redeemed us to God by thy blood out of every kindred, and tongue, and people, and nation;

Revelation 13:8: And all that dwell upon the earth shall worship him, whose names are not written in the book of life of the Lamb slain from the foundation of the world.

There is no doubt that the five principal offerings of the Old Testament economy were typical of the one perfect offering of Christ, and that each of the five sacrifices emphasizes a different aspect of the life and death of Christ for us. One offering would be inadequate to do this. (For explanations of each offering, see chapter 6.)

Type: Physical perfection of priests and animals

Leviticus 21:16–23, priests; *Leviticus 22:17–25, Deuteronomy 15:21 and 17:1* animals

Antitype: Christ's sinlessness

Hebrews 9:14: How much more shall the blood of Christ, who through the eternal spirit offered himself without spot to God purge your conscience from dead works to serve the living?

1 Peter 1:19: But with the precious blood of Christ, as of a lamb without blemish and without spot:

Both the priests and the animals used as sacrifices were typical of Christ; but they could not represent his sinlessness, because the priests, being men, had already sinned (Heb. 7:27) and animals are not capable of sin. Therefore, their physical perfection would typify Christ's sinlessness.

Type: Blood

Genesis 9:4: But flesh with the life thereof, which is the blood thereof, shall ye not eat.

Leviticus 17:11: For the life of the flesh is in the blood: and I have given it to you upon the altar to make an atonement for your souls: for it is the blood that maketh an atonement for the soul.

(Lev. 1:5, 3:2, 4:6–7, 7:2; 16:14)

Antitype: Efficacy of Christ's life and death

Matthew 26:28: For this is my blood of the new testament, which is shed for many for the remission of sins.

Hebrews 9:12: Neither by the blood of goats and calves, but by his own blood he entered in once into the holy place, having obtained eternal redemption for us.

Hebrews 9:22–23: And almost all things are by the law purged with blood; and without shedding of blood is no remission. It was therefore necessary that the patterns of things in the heavens should be purified with these; but the heavenly things themselves with better sacrifices than these.

1 John 1:7: But if we walk in the light, as he is in the light, we have fellowship one with another, and the blood of Jesus Christ his Son cleanseth us from all sin.

The shed blood of the animal sacrifices spoke of the efficacy of Christ's sinless life and death.

Type: Sin offering for the high priest and the congregation

(Lev. 4:3–12, 13–21; 6:30)

Antitype: Christ died for our sins outside of the gates of Jerusalem

Hebrews 13:11–12: For the bodies of those beasts, whose blood is brought into the sanctuary by the high priest for sin, are burned without the camp. Wherefore Jesus also, that he might sanctify the people with his own blood, suffered without the gate.

The sin offerings for the high priest and congregation were burnt outside the camp, instead of at the brazen altar, which typified Christ as our sin offering, who was taken outside the gates of Jerusalem to Golgotha to suffer.

Type: Day of Atonement

(Lev. 16)

Antitype: Efficacy of Christ as one sacrifice for the sins of the world

Hebrews 9:7–8: But into the second went the high priest alone once every year, not without blood, which he offered himself, and for the errors of the people: The Holy Ghost this signifying, that the way into the holiest of all was not yet made manifest, while as the first tabernacle was yet standing.

Hebrews 9:12: Neither by the blood of goats and calves, but by his own blood he entered in once into the holy place, having obtained eternal redemption for us.

Hebrews 9:25: Nor yet that he should offer himself often, as the high priest entereth into the holy place every year with the blood of others.

Hebrews 9:26: For then must he often have suffered since the foundation of the world; but now once in the end of the world hath he appeared to put away sin by the sacrifice of himself.

Hebrews 9:28: So Christ was once offered to bear the sins of many;

Hebrews 10:10: By the which will we are sanctified through the offering of the body of Jesus Christ once for all.

Hebrews 10:12: But this man, after he had offered one sacrifice for sins for ever, sat down on the right hand of God.

Hebrews 10:14: For by one offering he hath perfected for ever them that are sanctified.

The high priest could go into the holy of holies only once a year, on the Day of Atonement, with the blood to make atonement for the sins of the people. Likewise once, in the end of the world (Heb. 9:26), Christ died and shed his blood for the sins of the world, obtaining our eternal redemption. It should be noted that in Hebrews 9 through 10:20 the writer is speaking of the Day of Atonement; this fact is often overlooked.

Type: Veil

Exodus 26:33: And thou shalt hang up the veil under the taches, that thou mayest bring in thither within the veil the ark of testimony: and the veil shall divide unto you between the holy place and the most holy.

Leviticus 16:12: And he shall take a censer full of burning coals of fire from off the altar before the LORD, and his hands full of sweet incense beaten small, and bring it within the veil.

Antitype: Flesh of Christ

Hebrews 10:19–22: Having therefore, brethren, boldness to enter into the holiest by the blood of Jesus, By a new and living way, which he hath consecrated for us, through the veil, that is to say, his flesh; And having a high priest over the house of God; Let us draw near with true heart in full assurance of faith having our hearts sprinkled from an evil conscience, and our bodies washed with pure water.

The veil is closely associated with the Day of Atonement, which represents the efficacy of Christ's "one" sacrifice. The veil typified that this perfect sacrifice would not take place until Christ had come in the flesh to die.

As you can see, there are a variety of types associated with the tabernacle, but all relate to the fact that the tabernacle, and everything associated with it, is typical of the Gospel. This is why it is so important to stay within guidelines for interpreting a type. If we don't, we will miss this important fact. It is clear also that all that is typical is not given to us in detail in the antitype, as Hebrews 9:5 makes clear: "And over it the cherubims of glory shadowing the mercyseat; of which we cannot now speak particularly."

The furnishings, which represent Christ's ministries and sacrifice, are certainly typical, but which ministry of Christ does each item represent, and what is the meaning of the different sacrifices? It is at this point in interpreting the types of the tabernacle that we need to once again become cautious. The primary danger is behind us, because we have stayed within our guidelines and have seen in the antitype the areas of the tabernacle we should emphasize. Therefore, in the areas which are not clearly defined for us, we should not stress any new thoughts other than those which stay within the overall view of the antitype, and which are the obvious teachings about the gospel and Christ's ministries.

An example will demonstrate what I mean. As we have seen, the candlestick represents ministry of Christ, but often this is not where the emphasis is placed. The extremists often emphasize the gold, the number seven because of the seven stems, the bowls, knops, and flowers. Where are these things found in the antitype? The antitype of the tabernacle only emphasizes the candlestick as a ministry of Christ, nothing more. To place any emphasis on the design or material of the candlestick would lead us away from the intended meaning and destroy its relationship with the other items and the office of the high priest, which is paramount in understanding the true tabernacle as the gospel program.

It is important also to note that everything associated with the tabernacle does not have an antitypical meaning. This does not mean we cannot learn from these things. We need to interpret them as any other passage in the Bible. An example of this is the garments for the high priest, which are often interpreted as if they had an antitypical meaning. Why should this be done when there is ample explanation in Exodus 28 of the significance of each garment?

In the chapters on the outer court, holy place and holy of holies, we will learn in greater detail how the gospel is portrayed through the tabernacle, its furnishings, priesthood, and rituals.

PART 2

Panoramic View of the Tabernacle

Three basic concepts must be kept in mind as the last three chapters are read. First, the whole tabernacle typifies the gospel or plan of redemption. Second, the furnishings typify the ministries of Christ. Third, the high priest typifies Christ (see Chapter 5). If these three things are kept in mind, the harmony of the related types of the tabernacle and their clear fulfillment in the New Testament will be evident.

To simplify the teaching on the tabernacle, its furnishings, and the ministry of the high priest in the last three chapters, we can best understand them by examining the three major sections of the tabernacle separately: first, the outer court and its furnishings, which speaks primarily of sinners approaching a holy God through expiation of their sins; second, the holy place and its furnishings, which speaks of the ministries of Christ on behalf of those who experience forgiveness; third, the holy of holies and its furnishings, which reveals what was necessary for atonement.

To augment the lessons, one ritual pertaining to each chapter is described to further show its relationship to the New Testament.

The Court of the Tabernacle and its Offerings and Furnishings

"For it is not possible that the blood of bulls and of goats should take away sins" (Heb. 10:4).

The court of the tabernacle and its furnishings

117

The Brazen Altar

Many ancient peoples used altars. Although they were sometimes used for expiation of sin, most frequently their use deviated from this original purpose. Thus, idolatry and immorality are often associated with heathen altars.

For the Israelites, however, the sight of blood, fire, smoke, and the smell of burning sacrifices at the brazen altar impressed on them their guilt before God. Their altar was singularly a place of judgment and expiation for sin. The Israelites were not the first to understand this. From the beginning of man's rebellion this concept was established. In time, this idea was lost except to those who truly sought to please God. Nevertheless, the heathens continued to use altars because their conscience continued to witness their need for forgiveness. Thus, altars continued to be the means they employed to expunge their guilt, although they were used improperly.

When God revealed the pattern of the tabernacle, he continued to use the altar as a means of approach. To ensure that the Israelites worshiped only at the brazen altar and its service did not degenerate to the level of the heathen nations about them, he gave specific instructions for its use.

The most important instruction was that there was to be only one altar, (Exod. 27:1–8; 38:1–7) and it was to be located only in the court of the tabernacle (Lev. 17:1–9 and Deut. 12:5–14). This eliminated the spirit of divided worship that so characterized the common heathen worship on high places, which tended to encourage the concept of many gods. Therefore, all high places in the nation of Israel were to be destroyed (Deut. 12:1–4). Sacrificing to an idol carried the death penalty (Exod. 22:20).

One place of sacrifice for the nation made it easier for the priests to see that God's instructions were followed and so guarded against the influence of heathen worship. Divine instructions were very detailed in order to prevent any idolatrous deviations. The altar of the Lord was to have no engraving on it or steps to it as a precaution against the altar itself becoming an object of worship (Exod. 20:25–26) and the priests were to wear undergarments (Exod. 28:42) because God wanted no flesh exposed at his altar as was common at the heathen altars where nakedness and immorality abounded.

The Court of the Tabernacle and its Offerings and Furnishings

Some scholars have maintained that the instructions for altars in Exodus 20:25–26 were to be used in conjunction with those of the brazen altar in Exodus 27:1–8, but this is not so. Although the same instructions against steps or engravings would certainly be incorporated into the construction of the brazen altar, the altars in Exodus 20 were temporary altars made of earth or unhewn stone. Moses built a temporary altar according to these instructions after his fourth descent from Mt. Sinai when he offered burnt offerings and a sacrifice of peace offerings (Exod. 24:4–5).

Other times temporary altars were used are found in Joshua 8:30–31; Judges 6:24–32; 21:4; 1 Samuel 14:35; 2 Samuel 24:18–25; 1 Kings 18:30–35. There was also a prohibition against trees near the brazen altar (Deut. 16:21) because the heathen often worshiped in groves of trees and carved idolatrous figures out of them.

On the day that the tabernacle was set up, the brazen altar was placed in the outer court (Exod. 40:29), and all the tabernacle furnishings were anointed with holy anointing oil (Exod. 30:26–28, 40:9; Lev. 8:10; Neh. 7:1). A special anointing of the brazen altar continued for seven days, as did the priests' consecration (Exod. 29:35–37 and Lev. 8:11). The anointing was the ceremonial means of consecrating the altar and priests to their equally important work concerning atonement.

Also occurring concurrently with the consecration of the altar was its dedication by the people who were represented by their princes (Num. 7:1–3). This dedication lasted for twelve days (a day for each tribe), five days past the consecration of the altar. The solemn ceremony of the altar's consecration and dedication impressed on the people the sacredness God attributed to it.

The day after the consecration of the priests and brazen altar, the glory of the Lord appeared and his fire consumed the sacrifice on the brazen altar. The fire was a divine manifestation of his acceptance of the priests in their work at the brazen altar. It had the effect of causing the people to shout and fall on their faces (Lev. 9:23–24). No true Israelite would sacrifice on any altar but that of the tabernacle. The divine manifestation of fire, when Elijah challenged the false prophets of Baal and at the dedication of Solomon's temple, had a similar effect on the people (1 Kings 18:38–40 and 2 Chron. 7:3).

The laws governing the worship at the brazen altar and its impressive consecration and dedication were to instill on the priests and people their need for continuing obedience, which was the only real means of ensuring that at God's altar there would be no imitation of heathen practices. The many precautions the Lord took in keeping the altar free of heathen influences indicates that the altar was an important part of the Old Testament economy of worship. In fact, it was central to the whole system, for it was the place of atonement.

Altars have always been associated with access or reconciliation to God. The brazen altar's importance is signified by its position directly inside the entrance to the tabernacle. It was the only item of the tabernacle furnishings with which the offerer had any association. However, the offerer himself was not allowed to touch the brazen altar (Num. 4:15; 18:22). This association was vicarious through the animal sacrifice placed on the altar by the priest.

Though the offerer had no contact with the altar or other furnishings of the tabernacle (which typically represent the ministries of Christ), he received all of their benefits because he went to the altar. This is a fundamental truth concerning atonement. It is only when one recognizes his need for pardon and comes to the altar that he reaps the benefits of reconciliation. The brazen altar represented the place where expiation was appropriated by the offerer. It corresponds to the cross of the New Testament.

The Five Principal Offerings

The actual means of expiation is typified in the animal sacrifices at the brazen altar. Only the death of Christ, however, was actually accepted by God as truly expiatory (Heb. 10:4). Thus, to understand the importance of the brazen altar, we must also consider the animal sacrifices that occurred there, for they typified Christ's sacrificial death as the propitiation for mankind's sins.

Although there are no specific instructions concerning sacrifices in scriptural passages before the institution of the Levitical system, there are many passages that show that God's people were familiar with sacrifices. God clothed Adam and Eve in animal skins and presumably instructed them in the significance of sacrifices (Gen. 3:21). Cain and Abel, being instructed by Adam or God, continued to offer sacrifices (Gen. 4:1–4). Noah, (Gen. 8:20); Abraham, (Gen. 22:13–14); Jacob, (Gen. 31:54; Job 1:5); Moses,

(Exod. 3:18; 10:25) and Jethro, (Exod. 18:12) all seemed to have had knowledge about sacrifices before the Levitical system.

Although only two kinds of offerings were mentioned previous to the Levitical system, the burnt offering (Gen. 8:20, 22:2–13; Exod. 10:25, 18:12; Job 1:5, 42:8) and the drink offering (Gen. 35:14), more may have been known since the Hebrew word translated "sacrifice" in Genesis 31:54, 46:1; Exodus 3:18; 5:3, 8, 17; 8:8, 25–29; 10:25; 18:12 is a generic term.

The Hebrew words *zebach* and *zabach* are used in a general sense in these verses, meaning slaughtered animals. Later they were used primarily in connection with the peace sacrifice (Lev. 3:1, 9), associated offerings, thanksgiving sacrifice (Lev. 7:12–13), and vow sacrifice (Lev. 7:16 and Num. 15:3).

Another word for sacrifices was offering. Three Hebrew words are translated offering. *Qurban* is used in a general sense for blood or bloodless gifts brought to the altar. *Minchah*, with the exception of Genesis 4:3–4, is used exclusively for the meat offering. *Terumah* is used for gifts brought to the altar to be used in God's service, usually in association with the heave offering.

The greatest activity of sacrifices probably occurred at the time of the three harvests of Israel, which coincided with the national feasts (Lev. 23).

All males were required to come to the tabernacle at these times (Exod. 23:14–17, 34:22–23) and undoubtedly many individual offerings were made then in addition to the compulsory offerings of the nation when God promised special protection from invasion (Exod. 34:24). The number of animals sacrificed in the compulsory offerings throughout the year totaled at least 1,269, with thirty-two on the first day of the feast of tabernacles (see chart page 157). This was probably small in proportion to the offerings made on an individual basis.

As one reads the scriptures, it is easy to confuse the different offerings. Actually, there were only five principal offerings: sin, trespass, burnt, meat, and peace. The reason for confusion is often due to the other offerings associated with these five. They are the first-fruits, wave, heave, vow, voluntary or freewill, and drink offerings. These were offered by four classes of people: the priest, congregation, rulers, and the common person. They were offered daily, weekly, monthly, yearly, or whenever a need arose, all of

An Israelite brings his offering to the tabernacle

which makes it more difficult to distinguish one offering from another.

The five principal offerings, which are described in Leviticus 1—7, are often thought to have been used in the same order as given there, the burnt offering followed by the meat, peace, sin, and trespass offerings. In actual use, however, if they were all to be offered, the sin or trespass offering was offered first because expiation of sin is needed first. This was followed by the burnt, meat, and peace offerings (Lev. 9:1–22; 14:10–32; 16:1–24; Num. 6:9–17).

The five principal offerings can also be divided into two categories, the sweet and nonsweet savour. The burnt, meat, and peace offerings were called the sweet savour or pleasant odor offerings (Lev. 1:9, 2:9, 3:5; Eph. 5:2). This distinction is not because of any pleasantness in the smell of burning meat, but because they typically represented the absolute perfection and obedience of Christ.

The sin and trespass offerings were not called a sweet savour because God is not pleased with sin. This division is made clear in Numbers 15:1–12, which reveals that the sin and trespass offerings did not have an accompanying meat and drink offering, as did the other offerings. The fat of the sin offering mentioned in Leviticus 4:31 is called a sweet savour because the fat of any offering was a sweet savour (see Fat, page 125).

Just as God gave specific laws to govern the worship at the altar, he also gave specific instructions concerning which animals were to be offered there. A variety of animals were used in the sacrifices and offerings. They were oxen, sheep, goats, pigeons, and turtledoves. The term *herd*, or bevy, was used to designate the oxen. A common offering of the herd was a male calf called a bullock. The females were called heifers, cows, or kines. The flocks were the sheep and goats (Lev. 1:10). Kid goats refer to the male goats. Male sheep were called rams, and young sheep were called lambs or ewe.

The only fowls offered were turtledoves and pigeons. The turtledove was smaller than the pigeon, and common around dwellings, so it was more easily obtainable by the poor. All of these animals are similar in that they were domesticated and useful to man. These same animals are also mentioned in the Abrahamic covenant (Gen. 15:9–10).

All animals used in the sacrifices were edible, meeting the legal dietary conditions for clean animals: i.e. parting of the hoof and chewing of the cud, and so forth (Lev. 11:1–9; Deut. 4:3–8). Only perfect animals were acceptable since they represented a perfect sacrifice, like Christ's (Lev. 22:17–25 and Deut. 15:21, 17:1). The only exception to this was the freewill offering in which stunted or deformed animals were acceptable (Lev. 22:23).

All sacrifices had to be at least eight days old (Lev. 22:27d and Exod. 22:30). However, how old they could be is not specifically stated, although some set the age at three because that was the age of the animals offered in the Abrahamic covenant (Gen. 15:9–10). Nevertheless, Gideon was instructed by God to offer a young bullock that was seven years old (Judg. 6:25). It was prohibited to sacrifice both mother and offspring on the same day (Lev. 22:28). The common bloodless offering consisted of fine wheat flour.

A priest inspects a sacrificial offering

The Animal Parts of the Offering

It is easy to form a picture of the brazen altar as always heaped with animals. One may wonder how so many animals could be burned on an altar with a surface area of only 100 square feet. Actually, the only offering in which the whole animal was burned was the burnt offering. For the sin, trespass, and peace offerings, only the fat, blood, kidneys, and caul were offered on the brazen altar. A description of these specific parts follows.

In the Old Testament economy, the fat was regarded with as much sacredness as the blood (Lev. 3:17; 7:22–27), whereas in the New Testament, fat is not mentioned once, although blood continues to be of importance. The fat of any animal offered on the brazen altar was forbidden to be eaten, although it could be utilized in other ways. The penalty for eating the fat was for the offender to be "cut off from his people." A practical reason for burning fat was that it would fuel the fire and thus help to consume the rest of the offering.

The fat was from the covering of the inwards, or viscera, the kidney fat which completely surrounds the kidneys and the fat from the loins. Fat from these sources was primarily suet and easily removable. If the offering was a sheep, the rump and tail was also removed. On the rump and tail of the broadtailed sheep, a longtailed sheep of the Middle East, was a large deposit of fat, which sometimes weighed more than twenty pounds. This had to be cut off since it was not suet (Lev. 3:9).

Although there is no antitype for fat, it is obvious that fat represented perfection and good health in the sacrificial animal. God required the best for the offering simply because it typified Christ, the best of God. It is for this reason that the fat of a sin offering could be called a sweet savour even though the sin offering itself was not (Lev. 4:31). God was pleased with Christ as our propitiation, but not with the sin that he bore.

The laws governing the blood and its prominence during sacrifices indicate its tremendous importance. Depending on the offering and occasion, blood was applied to the mercyseat in the holy of holies, the inner veil, the horns of the incense altar in the sanctuary and on the altar in the outer court.

The methods of applying the blood, which could be as much as three gallons from a large animal, were sprinkling, putting (smearing), pouring, and strewing (also translated sprinkling). Only the sin offering had the blood sprinkled, put (smeared), or poured. All the other offerings were strewed. Sprinkling and smearing were always done with the fingers (Lev. 4:6, 17, 25, 30, 34; 8:15; 9:9; 16:14, 15, 18, 19) and not hyssop, which was used only in ceremonial cleansing (Lev. 4:4, 6, 49, 51, 52; Num. 19:6, 18; Ps. 51:7). The blood was sprinkled only at the mercyseat (Lev. 16:14,

15), and on the brazen altar (Lev. 16:18, 19) on the Day of Atonement, at the inner veil for the sin offering for the congregation and high priest (Lev. 4:6, 17), or on the side of the brazen altar when a bird was used by the poor for a sin offering (Lev. 5:9). At other times, the blood was "put" or smeared only on the horns of the brazen altar, for the sin offering of a ruler or common person (Lev. 4:25, 30, 34), Day of Atonement (Lev. 16:18) or on the horns of the incense altar for the sin offering of the high priest or congregation and Day of Atonement (Lev. 4:7, 18; Exod. 30:10). The remaining blood was poured out at the bottom of the brazen altar, probably on the inside, to facilitate drainage into the ash pans (Lev. 4:7, 18, 25, 30, 34). The blood at all other offerings was always sprinkled (Hebrew for *strew*) round about upon the altar (Lev. 1:5, 11; 3:2, 8, 13; 7:2). This, too, was probably applied to the inside of the altar so it could burn or drain into the ash pans.

The first biblical law regulating the use of blood is found in Genesis 9:4, which forbids the eating of any animal not well-bled, because life is in the blood. The same principle is established in the Mosaic law. The blood of any animal, sacrificial or not, was forbidden to be eaten (Lev. 3:17; 7:26–27; 17:10–16; Deut. 2:16, 23–25; 15:23. The penalty for eating blood was to be cut off from the nation. This penalty was well ingrained into Jewish consciousness. Thus, these regulations were incorporated into the early New Testament church (Acts 15:20) which was predominately Jewish, but were gradually dropped as the Gentile membership increased.

The statement in Leviticus 17:11 helps to explain the reason blood held such a significant part in the worship of the Old Testament economy: "For the life of the flesh is in the blood: and I have given it to you upon the altar to make atonement for your souls: for it is the blood that maketh an atonement for the soul." Since the blood is the literal vehicle of all life, whether animal or man, only it could adequately typify life, and give full meaning to God's provision for the expiation of our sins, as well as the efficacy of Christ's blood.

The kidneys are a vital organ of all higher life forms. They are necessary for the removal of waste products from the blood. Kidney can be translated *rein,* meaning the mind. Both kidneys of the sacrificial animals, along with all the fat that surrounded them, were offered on the brazen altar. Also offered was the caul, a small fold of fatty skin above the liver.

The Significance of the Offerings

For many, the sacrifices are confusing, but this confusion can be overcome by study. More confusing to modern believers is why God ever initiated animal sacrifices as a basic part of religion. Some would just say the law and tabernacle sacrifices have no meaning to present day believers and leave it at that. Others might say that the Old Testament is not important for us today. We need to understand that nothing God gives is imperfect. Let us remember that as a dispensation the Old Testament economy, with its animal sacrifices, was perfect (Rom. 7:12). Although it falls short of Christianity, it was this system that brought forth men like Abraham, Moses, Joshua, David, the prophets, and countless others.

The New Testament Christian sometimes overlooks the fact that God's method of entering into a covenant has always been by sacrifice. "Gather my saints together unto me; those that have made a covenant with me by sacrifice" (Ps. 50:5). Noah, (Gen. 8:20–21; 9:8–9); Abraham (Gen. 15:1, 2), and Moses (Exod. 24:5–8), all made covenants with God by sacrifices; but more important to us is that the New Testament was ratified by a sacrifice, just as the Old Testament was (Exod. 24:5). "And for this cause he is the mediator of the new testament, that by means of death, for the redemption of the transgressions that were under the first testament, they which are called might receive the promise of eternal inheritance" (Heb. 9:15).

The difference in animal sacrifices and the sacrifice of Christ is that his sacrifice was the only one that had any real efficacy in atoning for sin. The continual repetition of the animal sacrifices under the Old Testament economy is proof there was no efficacy in them. God never reveals why he waited until circa 33 A.D. for Christ to die for the sins of the world; he merely states, "But now once in the end of the world hath he appeared to put away sin by the sacrifice of himself" (Heb. 9:26).

Although the expiatory death of Christ took place thousands of years after mankind's original need for it, it was for the Old Testament saints as well as the New Testament saints (Rom. 3:25 and Heb. 9:15). How else could the Old Testament scriptures speak of their sins being atoned if this were not true (Ps. 103:3, Isa. 44:22 and Mic. 7:18–19)? Seeing that it would be a long time after man's need for pardon before it would actually be finalized, how could God reveal this principle to the Old Testament saints? Through animal sacrifice. Through a system of sacrifices God would educate his chosen people, and give them a shadow of his plan for their redemption.

Later, with the initiation of the Levitical system, he provided a deeper understanding of sacrifices than that of the pre-Mosaic times, it being of more doctrinal significance. Sacrifices were used to prefigure Christ's death for the Old Testament saints who could then, by faith, enter into a covenant relationship with God. Although there is no real atoning efficacy in these animals (Heb. 10:4), by faith they received the redemptive benefits of the actual sacrifice of Christ. The animal sacrifices served only as tangible means for the Old Testament saints to show their belief in and obedience to God's plan of redemption. Considering this, there is a remarkable statement in Hebrews 10:6 that is quoted from Psalm 40:6: "In burnt offerings and sacrifices for sin thou hast had no pleasure."

Although God certainly approved of animal sacrifices as a means prefiguring Christ's death, and as a means of revealing the faith of the Old Testament saints, we find God was not always satisfied with them. How are we to understand this, since God instituted animal sacrifices? As stated before, there was no efficacy in the animals sacrificed simply because they could never experience sin, and because animal sacrifices could not adequately reflect God's hatred for sin or his love for us. God could not accept them as real atonement, and therefore could not forget the offenses. "Wherefore when he cometh into the world, he saith, sacrifice and offering thou wouldest not, but a body hast thou prepared me" (Heb. 10:5). The blood of bulls and goats could never take away sin, although these sacrifices were sufficient to show the faith of the Old Testament saints in the coming redeemer. God accepted this faith, although the sacrifices never satisfied God's justice. Only after Christ had died and satisfied the demands of justice could there be final salvation. Thus, with Christ's death, there was no longer a need for a system of sacrifice, and it was done away with (Heb. 9:10; 10:1–9).

The fact that sacrifices were abolished has often led to a misunderstanding of their purpose and importance. Although animal sacrifices were inadequate for atonement of sin, they certainly must have been the best method possible to prefigure Christ, typify his sacrificial death, and reveal faith, or God would not have instituted them.

From man's viewpoint, animal sacrifices were unable to truly reflect his attitude toward God. However, this provided no problem for God who looks on man's heart (1 Sam. 16:7). It was obvious when the offerer purposely offered animals that did not meet the legal qualification, or knowingly failed to follow divine instructions, that his heart was not right. Of course, any such offering would not be accepted, as is the case in Genesis 4:3-7, 1 Samuel 15:22 and Malachi 1:6-10.

But what about the offerer who followed divine instructions? Was his offering automatically acceptable to God? No. Although obedience to the letter of the law can, to a certain degree, indicate the attitude of the offerer, it is in itself inadequate. Many times in Scripture the laws for offering were properly followed, but were not acceptable to God, because the heart of the offerer was not right (Prov. 21:3; Exod. 5:1; Isa. 1:11-18; Jer. 7:21-24; Hos. 6:6; Mic. 6:6-8; Mal. 3:3-4). Amos 5:21-24 exemplifies this truth:

> I hate, I despise your feast days, and I will not smell in your solemn assemblies. Though ye offer me burnt offerings and your meat offerings, I will not accept them: neither will I regard the peace offerings of your fat beasts. Take thou away from me the noise of thy songs; for I will not hear the melody of thy viols. But let judgment run down as waters, and righteousness as a mighty stream.

The writers of the above passages certainly understood that it was the proper attitude of their hearts that availed, and not the animal sacrifices.

David realized God was not interested in animal sacrifices, but rather the attitude of the heart or he could never have made the statement found in Psalms 51:16-19:

> For thou desirest not sacrifice; else would I give it: thou delightest not in burnt offering. The sacrifices of God are a broken spirit: a broken and a contrite heart, O God, thou wilt not despise. Do good in thy good pleasure unto Zion: build thou the walls of Jerusalem.

Then shalt thou be pleased with the sacrifices of righteousness, with burnt offering and whole burnt offering: then shall they offer bullocks upon thine altar.

The scribe in Mark 12:33 who questioned Jesus also realized it was the proper attitude of the heart and not sacrifices that availed.

Obedience to the moral law of God was paramount to the Old Testament economy, as it was with the new, because it reveals the true attitude of one's heart as long as the moral law is kept with regard to God. The system of sacrifices was added to teach the requirements necessary for pardon (Gal. 3:24). Obedience to the ceremonial laws of the sacrifices alone avails nothing, because it is not of faith. Conversely, obedience to the moral law alone is insufficient also, for salvation is not by works.

When the Israelites emphasized animal sacrifices alone, apart from obedience, they deserted the truth and purpose God had for them. Often the Israelites were willing to follow the ceremonial aspect of the law, but not the moral aspect. Although the sacrifices they offered typified Christ's death for their sins, they would not escape the penalty of the law on that account unless there was a subsequent repentance of sin. We can conclude that the animal sacrifices were only a temporary and tangible means by which Old Testament saints expressed their faith, in a substitute who would take away sins if the sacrifice came from a penitent heart sorry for breaking God's law.

We might wonder about the depth of meaning the Israelites associated with animal sacrifices. Did they know these sacrifices typified a man? Although this would not be necessary for their salvation, there is evidence that they knew this. The beautiful Messianic prophecy of Isaiah 53 reveals beyond a doubt that connection between the Levitical sacrifices and the Messiah, especially verses 5, 7, 10, and 11. Messianic prophecies up to this time were not as detailed or clear, and they could only be confirmed as Messianic until after Christ had come. Isaiah 53 was different in that it spoke of a man who was to suffer as a lamb and take away their sin. It would seem that all believing Jews from this time forward could form a concept of their Messiah as suffering a sacrificial death for their sins. Historically, Jews believed this to be a Messianic prophecy until sometime after Christ's death. The early church certainly viewed it as such. When Philip was asked by the Ethiopian, who was reading from Isaiah 53:7-8, "of whom speaketh the prophet of this? of himself or of some other man?" Philip preached unto him Jesus (Acts 8:34).

Another connection between the Levitical sacrifices and the Messiah is found in John 1:29: "The next day John seeth Jesus coming unto him, and saith, Behold the Lamb of God, which taketh away the sin of the world." John, being the son of a priest, would certainly be familiar with the Levitical sacrifices, and could not say this unless he realized its significance. Although there is no clear relationship between the Messiah and Levitical sacrifices, from what Simeon and Anna said in Luke 2:25, 30, 32, and 38, it is obvious they believed he was the Messiah. Simeon quotes from Isaiah 42:6, and was probably familiar with Isaiah 53 also, which the Jews universally held to speak of the Messiah as suffering as a lamb for their sins.

As we look at each of the offerings, keep in mind that they all represent various aspects of the life and death of Christ. One sacrifice would be inadequate to portray all the facets of his sacrificial work. Individually, each of the five offerings were in some way inadequate. It is only when they are viewed together that we have a complete picture of Christ as a sacrifice for our sins. Although it is certain the sacrifices are typical, we need to be careful in interpreting them, since there is little information given in their antitype. We should stress only the most obvious teaching about his life and death, and not seek to find meaning in every minute detail. We should also consider that since the brazen altar was the only item the offerer had any association with, it would be the means of expressing his needs and the attitudes of God. This indicates that we can learn two lessons from the offerings: how they relate to Christ and how they relate to the offerer.

To facilitate the reader in this study, general information concerning each of the five principal offerings is included on separate pages. This information will help the reader to quickly find the necessary factual information about each offering, and eliminate needless repetition of these facts.

The Sin Offering

The first sin offering took place during the consecration of Aaron and his sons to the priesthood (Lev. 8:14). No others are recorded before this. All of the other offerings were probably known before this time, although some are not mentioned specifically. The sin offering prefigured the atoning death of Christ. (Although the burnt offering also typified this aspect of Christ's death, it did not deal exclusively with atonement.)

With this specific offering, the nation had a fuller concept of the need for pardon: the stain of sin and its removal is the nucleus of theology. It is only through understanding the nature of sin that we can begin to understand and appreciate the tremendous measures God took to set mankind free from its penalty. The atoning death of Christ played the key role in providing the solution, because it was only through the vicarious death of Christ that God could wisely pardon mankind's sin. The sin offering points to this.

Of the five principal offerings, the sin offering is easiest to comprehend since there is much antitype information related to it. Considering the light the modern believer has about the atoning death of Christ, the sin offering seems only to cast a shadow of understanding. However, the Old Testament saints learned the elementary principles about the atonement from this offering which prefigured the death of Christ. Considering that one of the duties of the offerer when making a sacrifice was to personally kill the animal, he thus learned that sin brought death, revealing the wrath of God against sin and man's need for pardon.

The sin offering was always the first offering, because atonement was necessary before there could be further progress in a relationship with God through the other offerings. The importance of the sin offering above the other offerings is suggested in the special application of the blood of the sin offering (see Blood page 125). The fact that there was no prescribed meat or drink offering in conjunction with the sin offering discloses that sin separates one from God until pardon is secured.

It should be noted that the sin offerings on an individual level did not typify the single atoning death of Christ, but served only as the means to increase the person's faith in the efficacy of the atoning death (Christ's). In other words, the daily sin offerings did not typify Christ's sacrificial death with each offering in the Levitical system of worship. This was typified in the sin offerings on the Day of Atonement only, which was offered once each year (Heb. 9:25; 10:1–3). This is further demonstrated by the fact that in sin and trespass offerings only one animal could be offered, whereas in the others, multiple sacrifices were permitted.

Death and the shedding of sacrificial blood are prominent in both testaments. The shedding of blood was necessary to properly impress on the mind the result of sin, but it also taught that there is no such thing as degree of sin in God's mind. We note that animals used for the sin offering were not classified according to the sin committed, but to the effect a particular class of people would have on influencing others in iniquity, and the ability of the offender to provide a sacrifice.

A sin committed by the high priest required a more solemn and emphatic ceremony because of the real and typical significance of his position. Therefore, a more valuable animal was required and a special application of its blood in the sanctuary was necessary. To sin after a closer walk and greater knowledge of God is a less extenuating crime: therefore, the blood of the high priest's offering was brought closer to God's presence in the sanctuary. The fact that there was only one kind of sacrifice within each of the four classes of offerers of the sin offering proves they were not classified according to the sin committed.

By making the offering specific, according to the offerer's ability to secure a sacrifice, God demonstrated the possibility for all men, regardless of their position in life, to meet his provision of reconciliation. This would certainly have been hard to teach if God had required the poor to bring an expensive bullock for their sin offering.

Specific animals are a feature of only the sin and trespass offerings. The other offerings could typically teach their lesson best with a variety of animals. Another important consideration in making the offerings specific was to guard against the idea that sin could be atoned more fully with a more valuable animal. This would be a natural human assumption apart from God's revelation.

Although the wrath of God toward sin and his justice in the execution of the law's penalty is seen in the death of an animal, the love of God is also revealed in that he accepts the substitutionary sacrifice. The offerer could therefore realize that his sin brought death, and that he did not suffer the consequence of his sin.

How clearly this speaks of Christ who vicariously suffered the penalty of the law, and made it possible for God's justice to be upheld, even though the ones deserving its penalty were set free. The offerer's apprehension of this was directly in proportion to how clearly he saw the wickedness of his sin. If he saw clearly the wickedness of his sin, he would then see clearly the love of God in rescuing him from its penalty.

This is still true today. Those who consider sin as a trifling matter will see very little of God's love or their duty to repent. Since sin is the transgression of the law (1 John 3:4), the sin offering was calculated to bring the offerer back to a place of respect for God and his laws. Of course, this could happen only if the offerer made his sacrifice from a penitent heart.

The sin offering was instructed to be offered for sin through ignorance against any of the commandments of the Lord (Lev. 4:2, 13, 22, 27). The Hebrew word used here for ignorance does not mean lacking in knowledge, or else God would not hold any man accountable. The word means inadvertently. The idea is of carelessness, forgetfulness, or action without regard to God. Almost any sin could fall into this category. Numbers 15:22–29 also deals with sins of ignorance, but in the sense that we normally understand the word to mean lacking knowledge. With the tremendous number of laws given, and the logistics of their promulgation, God anticipated that there would be cases where true ignorance would lead to violation of them. God made provision for this. So here, God dealt with the sin of omission, and in Leviticus 4, he dealt with the sin of commission.

Sin offerings dealt with numerous types of sins (Exod. 21–23 and Lev. 18–22), but primarily for those where restitution could not be made, such as murder, parental disrespect, adultery, idolatry, secret sin, ceremonial defilement, and so forth. Lev. 5:1–4 deals with three specific cases where sin offerings were required: for not revealing the truth when under oath, touching something unclean, and a rash oath.

Only presumptuous sin was unpardonable (Num. 15:30). Though both Old and New Testaments provided mercy for sins of commission or omission, neither provided mercy for presumptuous sin. Presumptuous sin is sin committed with full knowledge of the wrong and an unwillingness to repent and admit guilt. The writer of Hebrews expresses it this way, "For if we sin willfully after that we have received the knowledge of the truth, there remaineth no more sacrifice for sins" (Heb. 10:26). Exodus 21:14

also stated that sin of this nature could not be pardoned by going to the brazen altar because there is no forgiveness possible for unrepented sin. Both Adonijah and Joab, who plotted to overthrow Solomon's kingdom, went to the altar for safety (1 Kings 1:50; 2:28). Both were executed by Solomon, Joab at the altar itself.

When we investigate how sin is handled in a court of law, we need to understand that the letter of the law makes no provision for mercy, whether human or divine. It can only condemn sin. The mercy of God extended to man did not spring from his law (Gal. 3:21). God had to send his only begotten son to be able to wisely pardon man.

In human government it is usually not wise to pardon criminals. The penalty of the law is enforced even if the criminal has sorrow for his crime, because execution of the penalty served to discourage lawlessness in others. This, of course, was true in the judicial system of the nation of Israel, but because pardon in God's kingdom could wisely be extended if there was godly sorrow for sin, God provided for sacrifices to be a part of Israel's judicial system.

Nevertheless, for sins that carried the death penalty, when committed presumptuously, the person was taken from the brazen altar (Exod. 21:14). However, there is no indication that after committing a death-penalty sin, when there was true repentance, whether a sacrifice was made or the person was still executed. In King David's case, he was not executed, but he did suffer other consequences (2 Sam. 12:13–14). In Achan's case, on the other hand, after confession he was executed (Josh. 7:24–25). In lesser crimes, sacrifices could be made, but the penalty was still enforced (see Trespass Offering).

Sin Offering

1. *References:* Lev. 4:1–5, 13, 6:25–30; 7:7; Num. 15:22–31.
2. *Offering:* Young bullock for high priest and congregation, Lev. 4:13, 14. Kid goat for rulers, Lev. 4:23. Kid goat, female, or lamb for common people, Lev. 5:6, or two turtledoves or two young pigeons, Lev. 5:7. $1/10$ ephah fine flour for very poor, Lev. 5:11.
3. *Quality of offering:* Animals, without blemish, Lev. 4:3, 23, 28, 32. Flour, fine, Lev. 5:11.
4. *Where killed:* Before the Lord, Lev. 4:4, 15. Same place

burnt offering killed, Lev. 4:24, 29; 6:25, which was on the north side of the brazen altar, Lev. 1:11.
5. *Who killed:* Offerer, probably assisted by the priest, Lev. 4:4 24, 29. If birds the priest did, Lev. 5:8.
6. *Laying on of hands:* Yes, Lev. 4:4, 15, 24, 29.
7. *God's portion:* Fat that covers and is upon the inwards, the two kidneys with the fat, and the caul of the animals were the Lord's, being burned on the brazen altar, Lev. 4:8–10, 19–20, 26, 31, 35. The remains of animals offered for the high priest and congregation were also the Lord's, being burned outside the camp in the place of ashes, Lev. 4:11–12, 21; 6:30. If birds were offered, both were burned on the brazen altar, one for the sin offering first, the other for a burnt offering, Lev. 5:7–10. If flour only, a handful was burned, but without oil or frankincense, Lev. 5:11–12.
8. *Priest's portion:* The remains of the offerings by the rulers and common people were to be eaten by the priests in the outer court, Lev. 6:26, 29. The remains of a sin offering of flour belonged to all the priests, since it would be dry, Lev. 5:13; 7:10.
9. *Offerer's portion:* none
10. *Application of blood:* Blood from the offering of the high priest congregation was sprinkled seven times before the inner veil of the sanctuary. Some was applied to the horns of the incense altar, the rest was poured out at the bottom of the brazen altar, Lev. 4:6–7, 17–18; 6:30. Blood of the animals offered by the rulers and common people was applied to the horns of the brazen altar, the rest was poured out at the bottom of the altar, Lev. 4:25, 30, 34. If birds, the blood was sprinkled on the sides of the brazen altar, the rest at the bottom of the altar, Lev. 5:9.
11. *Voluntary or compulsory:* Compulsory, Lev. 4:3, 14, 23, 28
12. *Sweet savour:* no
13. *Other instructions:* The sin offering, bird, had its head wrung off, but it was not divided. The other bird used as a burnt offering was treated as such, Lev. 5:7–10. The new commands for sin offering found in Num. 15:22–31 deal with the sin of omission. On a congregation level, the sin offering was a kid goat, and a burnt offering of a young bullock with its meat and drink offering.
14. *Reason for offering:* For personal or congregational sin.

The Trespass Offering

Some people have supposed that the scripture reference to the trespass offering begins at Leviticus 5:1. If this be the case, there is no clear distinction between the trespass and sin offerings. Actually, the first thirteen verses of Leviticus 5 are a continuation of the sin offering. The trespass offerings begin at Leviticus 5:14 and continue to Leviticus 6:7.

Taking this into consideration, there are some obvious differences between the two offerings. Although the trespass offering was like the sin offering in that it was expiatory, it differed in that there could be no efficacy in the offering until restitution was made. This is the chief distinguishing feature of the trespass offering. It seems that the trespass offering was most often used when there could be a monetary value assessed to the damage done, and where the law broken was not so fundamentally important for the well-being of the victim. This was not always the case (Lev. 14:12, 19:20–22).

Thus, in the sin offering, the substitutionary animal bore the full penalty of the offerer's sin, whereas in the trespass offering restitution was needed to satisfy God's justice. Restitution repaired the damage to the victim, but this alone could not satisfy God's broken law, so an offering was needed as well.

The trespass offering clearly typified Christ who redressed God for our trespasses.

For the trespass offering, only a ram could be offered, whether the offerer was poor or rich. This taught the offerer that his duty to redress wrong was not altered by his circumstances. This differs from the sin offering where the animal was according to the ability of the offerer to provide, even going as far as to allow a non-blood offering (Lev. 5:11). Multiple sacrifices were not permitted for the trespass or sin offerings as they were for other offerings.

Sacrifices played an important part in Israel's judicial system. Depending on the crime, a sin or trespass offering was offered, although both were also offered for sins which broke no civil law. This was calculated to teach that crime was not only against a neighbor, but God, too, by dishonoring his laws given on behalf of the nation. Since restitution was the most common penalty, the importance of the trespass offering is obvious. There was always a fifth added to the amount of restitution. If the offerer was only to repair the damage he had done he would have lost nothing. However, by paying a fifth more he learned that sin never profits. The sacrifice further taught the offerer that there was no virtue in his restitution. Therefore, he needed to make an offering for atonement.

The priests also played an important role in the judicial system by ensuring that the restitution was made according to the law, before the sacrifice was offered, and in estimating its value. Because the trespass offering was associated with the breaking of the law, it can be divided into two categories: those against God and those against man.

Trespasses against God are identified as those pertaining to holy things (Lev. 5:15). This would be failure to pay tithes, firstborn, firstfruits, vows, or redemption money for a firstborn child. The price of the trespass plus a fifth more would be given to the priest to make restitution before the offering of a ram for atonement.

Trespasses against man could include a variety of offenses, not all of which were civil. Four specific ones are listed in Leviticus 6:2–3. They are: lying about property in trust, lying about partnership, lying about stolen property, and lying about lost property. These certainly were not the only trespasses possible, just as those listed for the sin offering in Leviticus 5:1–4 are not the only sins that one can commit.

Because the civil code of Israel established specific restitutional payments for certain crimes (Exod. 22:1–4, 7, 9), the restitution plus a fifth was for these four trespasses as well as any other crimes that did not have specific restitutional amounts established. Those that did have an established restitution were more severe, because the crimes affected the livelihood of the people and their most valuable possessions, their oxen and sheep.

The trespass offering dealt mainly with physical injury or cases where a monetary value could be assessed for damages. Christians today are just as obligated to make restitution in such cases. Additionally, the teachings of Jesus extend the crime to damages beyond the physical to include those that damage the spiritual well-being of a person. These certainly are as great as trespass sins, and so need expiation also. Damages by anger, malice, and so forth, can often be more harmful than those of a physical nature, since the damage often is not as easy to detect or redress.

Trespass offering

1. *References:* Lev. 5:14—6:7; 19:20–22; Num. 5:5–8; Exod. 22:1–15; Lev. 14, 22:14–16.
2. *Offering:* Always a ram, Lev. 5:15; 6:6; 19:22; Num. 5:8, except for cleansing from leprosy, which required a lamb, Lev. 14.
3. *Quality of offering:* Without blemish, Lev. 5:15, 18; 6:6.
4. *Where killed:* On the north side of the brazen altar, Lev. 1:11; 7:2.
5. Who killed: Although not stated, probably the offerer assisted by the priest, as in the sin offering.
6. *Laying on of hands:* Not stated but there was confession of sin (Num. 5:7). Since it was for sin committed, like the sin offering, there probably was laying on of hands.
7. *God's portion:* The rump, and the fat that covers the inwards, the two kidneys, and the fat, and the caul were burned on the brazen altar, Lev. 7:3–5.
8. *Priest's portion:* The remains were for all priests, eaten in the outer court, Lev. 7:6.
9. *Offerer's portion:* None
10. *Application of blood:* Sprinkled on the altar, Lev. 7:2.
11. *Voluntary or compulsory:* Compulsory, Lev. 5:15, 18; 6:6; 19:21; Num. 5:7.
12. *Sweet savour:* no
13. *Other instructions:* Restitution was always made first.
14. *Reason for offering:* Much like sin offering, but made when restitution could be assessed.

The Burnt Offering

The burnt offering is one of only two offerings identified before the Levitical system of sacrifices was instituted. It may have been offered for expiatory purposes before the Levitical system, but with the institution of the sin and trespass offerings, this aspect, if it existed, ceased, and a new significance was adopted, giving it more specific typical meaning.

The burnt offering was probably offered for a variety of reasons, such as a need for renewed consecration because of sin, a change in circumstances enabling one to devote more to God, or an increase in moral knowledge.

Typically, the burnt offering represented the perfect and total consecration of Christ to God. This was indicated by the burning of the whole animal, its chief feature, on the brazen altar. The offering of only the fat, caul, and kidneys of the other offerings would not be adequate to represent total consecration.

The sacrificial animals of the burnt offering were more thoroughly examined and prepared than those of the other offerings, being flayed for a closer examination of blemishes. If none were found, the inwards and legs were washed, ceremonially signifying the animal was pure. If Christ had transgressed God's law, he would not have been a pure sacrifice acceptable to God, but the Bible declares that Jesus was without sin (Heb. 4:15) and did not sin (1 Peter 2:22). Thus, Christ's offering was a sweet-smelling savour (Eph. 5:2).

The "to make atonement" in Leviticus 1:4 does not refer to making atonement for sin as in the sin and trespass offerings. The offerer of the burnt offering approached God not as a sinner but as a saint, sin being forgiven with the sin or trespass offering. The offerer here identified himself with God in total consecration. As Christ's consecration to God made possible for him to remove the effects of sin in the world (atonement), so the consecration of the offerer to God made it possible for the removal of sin in his life (atonement). It was the perfect obedience of Christ that made his life acceptable to God as a sacrifice. Therefore, in the sacrifice of the burnt offering, it was the godly obedience of the offerer that kept him free from sin, and thus made him acceptable.

The Hebrew word for burnt offering is *Olah*, which means to ascend. Only the believer who has a consecrated life can be acceptable to God and ascend as a sweet savour (2 Cor. 2:15). Jeremiah spoke of a time when the nation of Judah no longer delighted in God's words and were disobedient to them (Jer. 6:10). God did not accept their burnt offerings. Let us not forget our duty to obey God, lest we find ourselves unacceptable to him.

The offering of the whole animal taught that every offerer must love God with all his heart, soul, mind, and strength; while the variety of animals that were acceptable taught that, regardless of circumstances or ability, everyone is capable of meeting this condition. It matters little to God that one may have 200 pounds of strength and another only 110, or one an I.Q. of 95 and another 135, because everyone is capable of devoting all they possess in their consecration to him. All God requires is all, anything less is no consecration. Paul was certainly thinking of the burnt offering when he said "present your bodies a living sacrifice, holy, acceptable unto God which is your reasonable service" (Rom. 12:1–2).

The variety of animals allowed in the burnt offering enabled the offerer to express value of his devotion to God, but at the same time, this also showed consideration for the poor who could not afford the more valuable animals. In such cases a dove offered by a poor person could be as great in God's sight as the thousand burnt offerings offered by Solomon (2 Chron. 1:6).

The burnt offering could also be offered both individually or corporately as the other offerings, but it was the only one that was offered on a daily basis. This speaks of continual consecration.

Burnt Offering

1. *References:* Lev. 1:1–17; 6:9–13; 7:8.
2. *Offering:* Bullock, male sheep, male goat, turtledove, or pigeon, Lev. 1:2, 3, 5, 10, 14.
3. *Quality of offering:* Without blemish, Lev. 1:3, 10.
4. *Where killed:* North side of the brazen altar, Lev. 1:11.
5. *Who killed:* Offerer, probably assisted by the priest, Lev. 1:5, 11, 12.
6. *Laying on of hands:* Yes, Lev. 1:4.
7. *God's portion:* All burned on the brazen altar, except the skin, Lev. 1:9, 13.
8. *Priest's portion:* Skin, Lev. 1:6; 7:8.
9. *Offerer's portion:* None
10. *Application of blood:* Sprinkle the blood on the brazen altar, Lev. 1:5, 11. If a bird, blood wrung out at the side of the brazen altar.
11. *Voluntary or compulsory:* Voluntary, Lev. 1:3.
12. *Sweet savour:* Yes, Lev. 1:9, 13, 17.
13. *Other instructions:* The animal's inwards and legs were washed in water, Lev. 1:9, 13. If a bird, the head was wrung off, crop and feathers plucked off and cast in the ashes; wings were cut off, but the body wasn't cut in two, Lev. 1:15–17.
14. *Reason for offering:* Made as a token of the total consecration of the offerer's life to God.

The Meat Offering

In reading chapter two of Leviticus, you will discover that this offering was actually flour or grain, and not meat as the name suggests. It is the only meatless offering, and thus the only bloodless offering of the five principal offerings of the Levitical system. Instead of the word *meat*, a better translation today might be food, meal, grain, or bread offering. The King James Version was written when the word *meat* was used more like we use the word *meal* today.

It cannot be determined from scripture whether or not this offering was offered independently of the other offerings. However, chapter 15 of Numbers definitely teaches that it always accompanied the other offerings, except the sin and trespass offerings. It also accompanied the offering of the national feasts. The meat offering was offered either baked or dry. Its description in chapter two of Leviticus gives no indication of the measure of fine flour offered in dry meat offerings. However, it is given in Numbers 15 along with the amount of oil and wine for drink offering. A drink offering always accompanied a meat offering. In Numbers 15, there is no mention of frankincense as in Leviticus 2 or the amount offered, although we know it was certainly offered.

The amount of flour, oil, and wine offered varied according to the kind of animal offered. The amounts are: for a lamb, $1/10$ ephah flour mingled with ¼ part of a hin of oil, and ¼ part of a hin of wine; for a ram, $2/10$ ephah flour mingled with ⅓ part of a hin of oil, and ⅓ part of a hin of wine; for cattle, $3/10$ ephah of flour mingled with ½ hin of oil and ½ hin of wine. These amounts were offered with each animal and not just once for the particular occasion. It should be noted that probably only a small amount of the oil was used either in the baked or dry meat offerings. What was not burned on the altar went to the priests (Lev. 2:2–3; 7:9–10). Although water is not mentioned, it was most probably added to the baked meat offerings since it is always necessary for baking.

In the burnt offering we see Christ's consecration as it was directed godward. Anyone familiar with the Ten Commandments knows that the first four relate to God and the last six relate to man, teaching that true godliness consists of consecration to both God and man. In other words, in order to have a proper understanding of our relationship and duty to our neighbor, it must be based upon a proper relationship to God. This is why the meat offering was with the burnt offering and not vise versa. In the meat offering, then, we see Christ in his service to man. Likewise, we too are to consecrate ourselves to serving other men. The meat offering, being bloodless, speaks of life and not death. Christ could have come and lived an obscure life and died for our sins, but how little man would have learned about God and godliness. What Christ showed us through his life and the words he spoke has become of infinite value to mankind. He left a perfect example for all men to follow, something law can only imperfectly teach, even though it is a perfect law.

The prohibition against the use of leaven, honey and the addition of salt, oil, and frankincense, and a drink offering to the meat offering, all teach other lessons of Christ's service to mankind, as well as our own.

Leaven is clearly typical of the evil effects of sin, no matter how little a sin we might believe it to be, whether corporate or individual, physical or mental. Both Christ and Paul used leaven to represent sin (Matt. 16:6, 11, 12; 1 Cor. 5:6–8). Leaven is a lump of dough that has been allowed to ferment. When only a small amount of leaven is mixed with new dough, it will produce fermentation of the whole amount. We see, then, why leaven was used to typify the pervading effects of sin, and why it was forbidden to be used in the meat offering, or offered on the brazen altar as a firstfruit offering.

Honey, for similar reasons, was also prohibited. It, too, is subject to fermentation. Honey may have also represented things of the world that in themselves are not sinful but, if overdone or not done with the right attitude, become sinful. Although a little honey is good, too much will sour the stomach (Prov. 25:27). Christ, although he never sinned, experienced the pressures and temptations of the many good things he could have done, which were out of the will of God.

The prohibition against leaven and honey extended only to their use at the brazen altar. Both could be offered, though not burned at the brazen altar as a firstfruit offering. Leviticus 2:12, which reads, "As for the oblation of the firstfruit" should read "as an oblation of the firstfruit" as in the American Standard Version.

Salt was to be cast on all offerings. The only instruction regarding it accompanies instructions for the meat offering. Because of this, some people have interpreted this to mean it applies only to the meat offering. Ezekiel 43:24 states that salt was cast on the burnt offering and, in Mark 9:49, Christ substantiates this more general use among all offerings. In the baked meat offering, salt was probably added as an ingredient.

Salt, unlike leaven, seasons, preserves, and helps control bacteria and fermentation, and its physical attributes are used in a spiritual sense in the New Testament (Matt. 5:13; Mark 9:50; Luke 14:34; Col. 4:6). How wonderfully this typifies Christ whose very life preserved life on this planet, and checked the corruption of sin.

Oil was another important factor ingredient of the meat offering. Anointing oil was used ceremonially as a means of consecrating a person to the work of God. Jesus was the anointed one whose anointing was by the Holy Spirit, which is the real oil used to consecrate a person to God's work (Luke 4:18). Christ began his public ministry with his baptism by the Holy Spirit. Just as the oil made the flour useful for baking, the Holy Spirit makes men useful for God's purpose.

The importance of frankincense is seen in its use as an incense typical of prayer (Ps. 141:2; Rev. 5:8; 8:3, 4). Frankincense can be understood to represent the prayers of Christ. Prayer was his invisible link to the Father from whom he drew his strength, his understanding, and his guidance.

The drink offering is not specifically described in any sacrifice, although Numbers 15 and other references state a drink offering was always offered with the meat offering (see Drink Offering page 154). The link between them is not clearly understood, but Moses called the juice of the grape blood (Deut. 32:14), which may indicate that wine was even then looked on as a symbol of blood, since the meat offering was the only bloodless offering, the drink offering, if symbolic of blood, would be a most logical and symbolic accompaniment. If so, the pouring out of the drink offering would teach of Christ, who by his blood (Lev. 17:11), poured out his life, not as an expiation but as a perfect example of a soul completely surrendered to God, that man may have a living, visible, and historical example to follow.

Christians, who are to emulate the life of Christ, are equally obligated to keep God's commandments as they relate to them and their neighbors. Thus, a Christian is to have no leaven (sin) in his life, and must be aware of too much carnal pleasure (honey). His life must be above reproach, making the world ashamed by his good works (salt). It must be a life full of the Holy Ghost (oil) to make it usable for the master's service, and must be a life of prayer, seeking to know God's will (frankincense). He must also pour out his life, completely surrendering to God's will, and love his neighbor as himself (drink offering).

Although these things can be understood by us today, for the Old Testament saint the meat offering represented something quite different. The presentation of the products of the earth, man's first food (Gen. 1:29), was given as a gift of homage, acknowledging God's sovereignty over all that is needed to sustain life.

Thus, while the burnt offering taught the Old Testament saints their need for total surrender and consecration of God, the meat offering complemented this by teaching that he would sustain them if they consecrated themselves to him. (See Table of Shewbread, page 165, for a more complete explanation.) We see this expressed in Joel 1:10, 11; 2:14. Joel recognized that it was God who made it possible for the earth to produce the wheat and wine needed to sustain man. The meat offering aptly represented this.

Firstfruits were also classified as a meat offering (Lev. 2:14–16). All produce from the earth was to be offered as a gift of homage to express reliance on God. This included barley and wheat (corn), wine, oil, honey, leaven, and dough (2 Chron. 1:5; Lev. 2:11–12; Num. 15:20). Firstfruits were offered on a corporate as well as an individual level (Lev. 23:9–14; Deut. 26:1–11), although on a corporate level it was always an offering of barley. Deuteronomy 26:1–11 teaches that while a basketful of the firstfruits was offered, only a memorial was actually burned on the brazen altar (Lev. 2:16). A memorial was a small amount, usually a handful, to represent the whole. The significance of the firstfruit offering is that Christ was said to be the firstfruit of them that slept (1 Cor. 15:20). Therefore, while the firstfruit represented the whole harvest, it also served as a promise that the rest of the harvest was God's. In the same way, Christ was the firstfruit of the church, and our guarantee that the entire church shall be redeemed and resurrected.

Meat Offering

1. *References:* Lev. 2:6; 14–16; 7:9–10; 10:12–13.
2. *Offering:*

A. Uncooked fine flour with oil and frankincense, Lev. 2:1–3.
　　　B. Cakes, baked in an oven, cooked on a griddle (pan) or a frying pan. All were to be mingled with oil with no leaven, Lev. 2:4–7.
　　　C. Firstfruits as a meat offering. The grain was parched and beaten with oil and frankincense (see firstfruit offering), Lev. 2:14–16.
3. *Quality of offering:* Fine flour, Lev. 2:1, 4, 5, 7.
4. *Where killed:* N/A
5. *Who killed:* N/A
6. *Laying on of hands:* N/A
7. *God's portion:* Always a handful with some of the oil but all of the frankincense. If cakes, a small portion called a memorial, Lev. 2:2, 9, 16; 6:15. All was burned on the brazen altar, Lev. 2:9; 6:15.
8. *Priest's portion:* Remainder of all meat offering, Lev. 2:3, 10; 6:16–18; 10:12. All dry meat offerings were for all the priests, Lev. 7:10. Cakes went to the officiating priest Lev. 7:9. All meat offerings were to be eaten in the outer court, Lev. 10:12–13; Num. 18:9–10.
9. *Offerer's portion:* none
10. *Application of blood:* N/A
11. *Voluntary or compulsory:* Voluntary, Lev. 2:1, 4, 5, 7, 14.
12. *Sweet savour:* Yes, Lev. 2:2, 9.
13. *Other instructions:* Leaven was forbidden to be used in any meat offering, Lev. 2:4, 5, 11; 10:12 or burned on the brazen altar, Exod. 23:18; 34:25; as was honey, Lev. 2:11; although these could be offered as firstfruits, Lev. 2:11–12. Salt was to be added to all offerings, Lev. 2:13; Ezek. 43:24; Mark 9:49.
14. *Reason for offering:* Made as a token of the offerer's life to his fellow man.

The Peace Offering

The chief feature of the peace offering was the festive meal, shared by God, the priests, and offerer (1 Sam. 1:4, 5). In the other offerings, various portions went to either God or the priests, but never to the offerer. The peace offering was always offered last when offered with the other offerings, although it could be offered by itself. The peace offering was not offered to appease an angry God, but rather with the desire to express a feeling of peace after a person experienced pardon, and had consecrated their life to God. Thus, the peace offering was not offered by someone seeking peace, but by someone in a state of peace. The peace offering as always laid on the burnt offering (Lev. 3:5; 6:12), teaching that only a consecrated life can lead to peace. This typified Christ in that it portrays his expiatory death by which peace, reconciliation, and communion with God are possible.

God's portion was specifically called food in the peace offering. The reason the term *food* is used with regard to God's portion of the peace offering was to distinguish it from the priest's and offerer's portion. One may take this to have some special significance since it related to only the peace offering, but the same word is translated bread in Leviticus 21:6, 8, 17, 21, 22; 22:25 and Numbers 28:2.

We learn from Leviticus 21:22 that this bread (food) of God was divided into two categories, "most holy" and "holy." "Most holy" refers to the meat offering (Lev. 7:1) and the shewbread (Lev. 24:9). The priests received a portion of God's "most holy" food, because they were his representatives. It could be eaten only in the outer court (Lev. 6:16; 24:9; 7:6 and Num. 8:10). God's portion was burned on the brazen altar. "Holy" refers to the heave and wave offerings of the peace offering, firstfruits, firstborns, and devoted things (Num. 18:11–19), which are primarily for the priests. They were permitted to be taken from the tabernacle.

The particular portions of the peace offering given to the priests were called the wave-breast and heave-shoulder. These portions were appointed by God for the priests at the time of their consecration at the priest's office (Exod. 29:28). The wave-breast, which was probably the shoulder portion, was presented to the Lord with a side to side swinging motion, while the heave-shoulder, which was probably the thigh of the animal, was moved upward and downward during its presentation. Only the right shoulder was offered in the heave offering (Num. 18:18; Lev. 7:32; 8:25, 26). It went to the officiating priest (Lev. 7:33). The presentation movements were to indicate the offerer's consecration to God, although the portions were not burned on the altar.

The wave offering seemed to have been of lesser importance than the heave offering. Although it was shared by all priests, it was never associated with any offering mentioned other than for the peace offering, whereas the heave offering was used as booty (Num. 31:29), firstfruit (Num. 15:19–21), and tithes (Num. 18:24–28). The heave and wave offerings were the priest's portions to be shared with their families (Num. 18:11). After God's portion, the fat, kidney, and caul, were burned on the brazen altar, and the priest's portions, the shoulder and right thigh, were divided. The remaining parts went to the offerer and his family to feast on in the court of the tabernacle (Lev. 7:15–16; 1 Sam. 1:4).

There were a variety of animals that were offered as peace offerings, like the burnt offering, making it possible for the poor to express their degree of thankfulness to God. This could be further expressed by offering any number of animals, such as Solomon who offered 22,000 oxen and 120,000 sheep at the dedication of the temple (1 Kings 8:63). Birds were excluded from the peace offering because they were too small for a feast, and thus were unable to teach friendship, fellowship, and communion.

There were three types of peace offerings; the thanksgiving, the vow, and the freewill. The Hebrew word for peace offering means "to give in return," which is well-characterized by these three kinds of offerings. The circumstances and attitude of the offerer determined which one of the three offerings were used.

The thanksgiving offering was offered in retrospect for God's "past" goodness, in forgiveness for sin, and in protection from enemies or natural afflictions. This attitude is beautifully expressed in Psalms 107:19–22 and 116:9–17.

Vow offerings were offered only after certain conditions of a previous vow were fulfilled. A vow usually accompanied a prayer during times of sickness or distress. The vow itself was not made in hopes of enticing God to answer a prayer, but if the needs were met, the vow offering would be given in thanksgiving (Gen. 28:20–22; Judg. 11:30–31; 1 Sam. 1:11). The offerer could vow anything he owned, such as persons, animals, houses, or lands. These things were then to be used in the service of God. Although vows were made on a voluntary basis, once vowed, the person was obligated to complete the pledge (Eccles. 5:4–6; Deut. 23:21), unless abrogated legally as stated in Numbers 30.

If a person was vowed, he was to be redeemed. Vowing a person was actually an act of vowing a given amount of silver, which was given to a priest. The amount of silver for a vowed person was set according to age; one month old to five-year-old males, five shekels, females, three shekels; five-year-old to twenty-year-old males, twenty shekels, females, ten shekels; twenty-year-old to sixty-year-old males, fifty shekels, females, thirty shekels; sixty-year-old and above males, fifteen shekels, females, ten shekels (Lev. 27:1–8).

Animals, houses, and lands could also be redeemed at their estimated value, plus a fifth.

The nature of the free will offering, which was called a voluntary offering in Leviticus 7:16, is that of spontaneous thankfulness. It was different from the thanksgiving offering in that it was not in recognition of some specific past goodness of God, and it was distinguished from the vow offering in that nothing had previously been vowed. The Hebrew word for this offering means "spontaneous," which characterizes its nature as springing naturally from the believer's heart.

Peace Offering

1. *References:* Exod. 29:26–28; Lev. 3; 7:11–21, 28–36; 10:14–15; 19:5–8; 22:21–23, 29, 30; Deut. 18:3.
2. *Offering:* Ox, male or female; sheep, male or female; goats.
3. *Quality of offering:* Without blemish, Lev. 3:1, 6; 22:21–22. Stunted or deformed animals were allowed for freewill offerings, Lev. 22:23.
4. *Where killed:* At the door of the tabernacle of the congregation or north side of the brazen altar, Lev. 3:2, 8, 13; compare with Lev. 1:5, 11.
5. *Who killed:* Offerer, probably assisted by the priest, Lev. 3:1, 2, 8, 13.
6. *Laying on of hands:* Yes, Lev. 3:2, 8, 13.
7. *God's portion:* Fat that covers and is upon the inwards, two kidneys and its fat, and the caul (the rump of a sheep), Lev. 3:3, 4, 9, 10, 14, 15. Probably a memorial of the unleavened wafers and cakes, Lev. 7:12.
8. *Priest's portion:* The breast, which was waved for a wave offering, went to the priests, and the right shoulder, which was heaved as a heave offering, went to the officiating priest, Lev. 7:31–36; Exod. 29:26–28. The officiator also received one of the leavened breads used in the offerer's meal, and probably the remains of the unleavened wafers and cakes,

Lev. 7:9, 12–14. The priest's portion of the peace offering could be shared with his family, Lev. 10:14; Num. 18:11. If Deut. 18:3 applies to the peace offering, then the officiating priest would also receive, besides the shoulder, the two cheeks and maw, or stomach.

9. *Offerer's portion:* He would receive the remains of the animal and leavened bread to be eaten before the Lord. If a thanksgiving offering, the meal must be eaten the day it was offered. If a vow or voluntary, then it could be eaten the second day but not the third. If any was left it was to be burned, Lev. 7:14–18; 19:5–6; 22:29–30.
10. *Application of blood:* Sprinkled on and round about the altar, Lev. 3:2, 8, 13.
11. *Voluntary or compulsory:* Voluntary, Lev. 19:5; 22:29.
12. *Sweet savour:* Yes, Lev. 3:5, 16.
13. *Other instructions:* The peace offering was of three kinds; thanksgiving, Lev. 7:12–15; vow and voluntary, commonly called freewill, Lev. 7:16. Anyone who was unclean through disease or contact with something unclean and partook of the peace offering was to be cut off from his people, Lev. 7:20–21.
14. *Reason for offering:* To symbolize the fellowship between God and his people.

The Ritual of the Sin Offering

Normally an Israelite's first act in making a sin offering was to select the appropriate animal. If he was not of the proper class, he would select a lamb or female goat and bring it to the gate of the tabernacle. This was a solemn act and not done in a casual manner. Although the offerer had already sensed his separation from God, as he neared the tabernacle and saw the linen curtain, the gate, the priests, the veil, fire, and smoke at the brazen altar, he could hardly fail to recognize, in greater measure, how great his separation really was; sin was not a simple matter to deal with. The offerer became aware that there was an elaborate and detailed method for atoning for sin. At the same time, however, he saw the priest as a mediator who could go before God on his behalf, while the perpetual fire (Lev. 6:13) spoke to him of access to God at any time.

At the gate of the tabernacle (A), the priest would question him

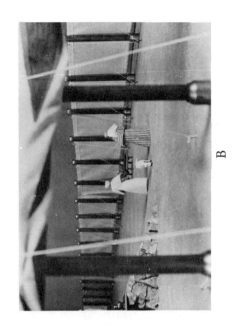
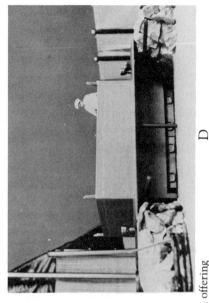

The ritual of the sin offering

as to what kind of offering was to be made, and examine the animal to be sure it was without blemish (typifying Christ's sinlessness). The offerer was then led to the north side of the altar where he laid his hands on the head of the animal and confessed his sins (B).

Confession was an important part of the Old Testament economy (C), as it is under the new (Lev. 5:5; 16:21; Num. 5:7; Neh. 1:6; Rom. 10:9; 1 John 1:9; James 5:16). Confession was not to inform God of the wrong that had been committed; rather it served to make the offerer properly acknowledge his sin, just as God's interrogation of Adam was not because of his ignorance, but rather it was to get Adam to confess what he had done (Gen. 3:9–12).

The ritual of the sin offering helped the offerer to demonstrate through his actions two things: his awareness of his guilt and his need of obedience to God's plan for removal of the penalty of sin. These two things are essential for the New Testament saint as well.

The offerer was responsible for killing the lamb, but he was probably assisted by the priest who would catch the blood in a bronze bowl. When the offerer put the knife to the animal's throat, the blood would gush out, and the animal would die a struggling death. We should not underestimate the effect this had on the offerer, how clearly this taught the offerer his responsibility for his own sins. The scene was an object lesson teaching that sin brings death, and that the one who deserves the full wrath of God lives at the expense of another. How clearly this portrays Christ, whose shed blood and death once and for all atoned for mankind's sins.

While the offerer was busy cutting the fat, kidneys, and caul from the animal, the priest took the blood, after washing at the laver, to the brazen altar (D). There he smeared some of the blood on the horns and poured the rest out at the bottom of the altar. The smearing of the blood on the horns of the altar may have represented its expiatory power, since in Amos 3:14, the altar was made useless after the horns were cut off. The blood, which is the life (Lev. 17:11) being poured out, represents Christ's life poured out for our sins. The sin offering was the only offering in which the blood was applied in this manner. The priest again washed at the laver before taking the fat, kidneys, and caul and burning them at the altar.

The priest who mediated on behalf of a man could not, in himself, typify the shedding of blood and death of Christ. However, the animal sacrifice did. Thus, both priest and the offering expressed typically Christ as mediator and offering. Afterward, the offerer, then free from guilt, might have offered a burnt offering to express his renewed dedication, and a thanksgiving offering in recognition of God's mercies.

Tithes, Firstfruits, and Firstborn as Offerings

The firstfruit, firstborn (Exod. 13:2, 12, 29; 23:19; 34:26; Lev. 27:26; Num. 3:13; 15:17–21; 18:12–15; Deut. 6:1–11) and the tithes (Lev. 27:30–33; Deut. 12:17–18; 14:22–23) all belonged to God. The tithes of the nation of Israel consisted primarily of their crops and animals, since coins were not in use until a later time. The tithes went to the Levites who would then tithe of this to the priests. Only the firstfruit and firstborn went directly to the priests (Num. 18:12–28).

Although these offerings belonged to the priests and Levites, from them the offerer and his family were to enjoy a festive meal before the Lord during the national feasts (Deut. 12:5–7, 17, 18; 14:23, 26, 15:19–20). If the distance from the tabernacle prohibited bringing the offerings, they were to exchange them for silver, which would be used on their arrival to buy food for the festival. After the firstborn animal and firstfruits were offered at the brazen altar, the offerer's portion of the firstborn offering, which was treated like a peace offering (Num. 18:17–18), along with part of the tithes, were used to maintain the offerer and his family while at the feast. These served to offset the cost of the journey and food and to encourage participation in the feasts which coincided with the harvest season. All males were required to attend (Exod. 23:17; 34:23; Deut. 16:16).

It should be noted that both the firstfruit offerings and the tithes were called heave offerings (Num. 15:19–21; 18:24–28). Even the booty from the Midianites, which was given to Eleazar, was called a heave offering (Num. 31:29). Heave offerings were gifts presented to God in which none or only part of the offering was burned on the brazen altar, the rest being used in his service. The material used for the construction of the tabernacle was a heave offering (Exod. 25:2, 9). There was also a regular heave offering with the peace offering, which should not be confused with these (see Peace Offering, page 146).

Drink Offering

The drink offering is one of only two pre-Mosaic offerings mentioned by name (Gen. 35:14). With the institution of the Levitical offering it became part of it. The drink offering was used in all the offerings of the feasts as well as daily, weekly and monthly offerings (see offering chart page 155) and individual offerings since it always accompanied the meat offering (Num. 15:1–12).

The amount of wine offered varied, not according to the kind of offering but according to the kind of animal used. The amount of wine for each lamb or kid was ¼ hin, for each ram ⅓ hin, and for each bullock ½ hin, one hin being six quarts or 1½ gallons.

The flagons, or covers, kept at the table of the shewbread, were probably used for the drink offerings (Exod. 25:29). Numbers 28:7 states the drink offering was to be poured out in the sanctuary, although it was forbidden to be poured out at the incense altar (Exod. 30:9). Considering the amount of wine that would be poured out, the sanctuary seems to be an unlikely place. Many believe it was poured out at the brazen altar. This seems to be a more logical place considering that drink offerings were always offered with a meat offering, which was burned on the brazen altar. There the heat dissipated the moisture. The term *holy place* in Numbers 28:7 may refer to the outer court as it did in Leviticus 10:18 (compare with Lev. 6:26), which would then make reference to the brazen altar as the place it was poured out.

The significance of the drink offerings may be found in that it was always offered with the meat offering, a bloodless offering (see Meat Offering page 142).

The Laver

There are many opinions concerning the typical significance of the laver. Some Christians believe it represents the believer's water baptism, others the believer's sanctification, and others the word of God. Before we consider the significance of the laver, remember I have stressed that each furnishing represents a ministry of Christ. However, I believe the laver departs from this principle dramatically in that it also represents the innate sinless

Table 6 **The Compulsory Offerings for the Nation of Israel**

Frequency	Description	Burnt	Meat	Drink	Sin	Peace
Daily morning and evening	Continual burnt offering Exod. 29:38-42; Lev. 6:8-18; Num. 28:3-8	Two lambs one morning one evening	1/10 part of an ephah of fine flour mingled with 1/4 hin of beaten oil for each lamb.	1/4 hin wine for each lamb		
Weekly	Weekly sabbath burnt offering besides the continual burnt offering. Num. 28:9-10	Two lambs probably one offered in the morning the other in the evening.	2/10 deal (ephah) flour mingled with 1/4 hin oil Probably half in the morning and half in the evening. Num. 15:4	1/4 hin wine for each lamb. Num. 15:5		
Monthly	Monthly burnt offering besides the continual burnt offering. Num. 28:11-15	two young bullocks one ram seven lambs	3/10 deal (ephah) flour for each bullock 2/10 deal (ephah) flour for the ram 1/10 deal (ephah) flour for each lamb Flour mingled with oil Num. 15:4, 6, 9	1/2 hin wine for each bullock 1/3 hin wine for the ram 1/4 hin wine for each lamb	one kid goat	
Yearly	Passover First month, fourteenth day. Exod. 12:1-14, 21-27; Lev. 23:5; Num. 28:16; Deut. 16:1-2				male goat or sheep	
Yearly	Feast of unleavened bread. First month, fifth day to the twenty-first day. Offered each day besides the continual burnt offering. Exod. 12:15-20; Lev. 23:6-8; Num. 28:17-25; Deut. 16:3-8.	two young bullocks one ram seven lambs	3/10 deal (ephah) flour for each bullock 2/10 deal (ephah) flour for the ram 1/10 deal (ephah) flour for each lamb flour mingled with oil Num. 15:4, 6, 9	Those prescribed in Num. 15:5, 7, 10 were probably offered.	one goat	

Frequency	Description	Burnt	Meat	Drink	Sin	Peace
Yearly	Feast of Firstfruits (barley) First month, sixteenth day. Lev. 23:9-14.	He lamb or ram	Sheaf of the firstfruit ²/₁₀ deal (ephah) flour mingled with oil. Num. 15:16	¼ hin wine		
Yearly	Feast of Pentecost fifty days after firstfruit feast. Lev. 23:15-21; Num. 28:26-31; Deut. 16:9-21. Besides the continual burnt offering.	two young bullocks one ram seven lambs	New meat offering of ²/₁₀ deal (ephah) flour with leaven for firstfruit (wheat) ³/₁₀ deal (ephah) flour for each bullock ²/₁₀ deal (ephah) flour for the ram ¹/₁₀ deal (ephah) flour for each lamb. flour mingled with oil Num. 15:4, 6, 9	Those prescribed in Num. 15:5, 7, 10 were probably offered.	one kid goat	two lambs
Yearly	Feast of Trumpets Seventh month, first day Besides the continual burnt offering and monthly burnt offering Lev. 23:23-25; Num. 29:1-6	one young bullock one ram seven lambs	³/₁₀ deal (ephah) flour for the bullock ²/₁₀ deal (ephah) flour for each ram ¹/₁₀ deal (ephah) flour for each lamb. flour mingled with oil Num. 15:4, 6, 9	Not mentioned but probably those prescribed in Num. 15:5, 7, 10 were offered.	one kid goat	
Yearly	Day of Atonement Seventh month, tenth day Besides the continual burnt offering. Lev. 16; 23:27-32; Num. 29:7-11	one young bullock one ram seven lambs one ram one ram	³/₁₀ deal (ephah) flour for the bullock ²/₁₀ deal (ephah) flour for each ram ¹/₁₀ deal (ephah) flour for each lamb. flour mingled with oil Num. 15:4, 6, 9	Not mentioned but probably those prescribed in Num. 15:5, 7, 10 were offered.	one kid goat one young bullock two kid goats	

Frequency	Description	Burnt	Meat	Drink	Sin	Peace
Yearly	Feast of Tabernacles Seventh month, fifteenth day, for seven days, the eighth day a sabbath. Besides the continual burnt offering. Lev. 23:33-36; Num. 29:12-38; Deut. 16:13-15	First day 13 young bullocks 2 rams 14 lambs Second day 12 young bullocks 2 rams 14 lambs Third day 11 young bullocks 2 rams 14 lambs Fourth day 10 young bullocks 2 rams 14 lambs Fifth day 9 young bullocks 2 rams 14 lambs Sixth day 8 young bullocks 2 rams 14 lambs Seventh day 7 young bullocks 2 rams 14 lambs Eighth day 1 young bullock 1 ram 7 lambs	3/10 deal (ephah) flour for each bullock 2/10 deal (ephah) flour for each ram 1/10 deal (ephah) flour for each lamb flour mingled with oil Num. 15:4, 6, 9	Those prescribed in Num. 15:5, 7, 10 were probably offered.	one kid goat each day	

perfection of Christ rather than his ministry. Yet, it remains a ministry for the priest. Christ's moral perfection is something we can only inadequately grasp. We will only know him as he really is in some future time. Likewise, the laver has its mysteries. For instance, unlike the other furnishings there is no mention of accompanying utensils, bars or staves, no covering, and no indication of its size or shape.

Another basic fact concerning any typological application of the furnishings is that there is no antitypical information about how they represent the ministries of Christ. Therefore, the typological significance of the furnishings can be based only on Old Testament Scriptures and how they relate the item to the work of the priest, who typified Christ. Only the most obvious meanings should be taught, and those kept within the guidelines of the tabernacle as being representative of the gospel and the high priest as representative of Christ.

Exodus 30:19–21 is the only significant passage of scripture dealing with the laver. It is not referred to in the New Testament.

> For Aaron and his sons shall wash their hands and their feet thereat: When they go into the tabernacle of the congregation, they shall wash with water, that they die not; or when they come near to the altar to minister, to burn offering made by fire unto the Lord: So they shall wash their hands and their feet, that they die not: and it shall be a statute for ever to them, even to him and to his seed throughout their generations.

It is apparent that the penalty of death for not washing at the laver indicates its importance. Because the priest had to wash each time he ministered at the brazen altar or went into the sanctuary, he washed throughout the day.

There are many reasons for this. A practical reason, and one I am sure God took into consideration, was protection from disease. The priest's hands would become soiled from the blood while offering animals on the altar and his feet dirty from the earth floor of the outer court and sanctuary (Num. 5:17). Hands and feet are often the means of spreading and contacting disease, so the caution "that they die not" could apply to the practical necessity of preventing deadly disease.

However, the significance of washing elsewhere in the Old Testament reveals the importance of washing at the laver. Washing with water played an important part in cleansing from physical defilement (Lev. 11), disease (Lev. 13–15), death (Num. 19), and ceremonial defilement (Lev. 16:4, 24, 26, 28). The law encouraged the idea of a relationship between these things and sin, whereby washing played a part in its removal.

This same principle will help us understand the significance of the ministry of the priests at the laver. In what way did the washing at the laver affect the priests? It made it possible for them to minister at the brazen altar and in the sanctuary. Without washing they could not mediate for man in either place. Therefore, washing at the laver can only represent what made it possible for Christ to mediate for man. Only one thing would have kept Christ from being able to mediate for man, and that would be sin in his life. If he would have sinned once, his death on Calvary would have availed nothing. He would not have been resurrected, nor would he have ascended to heaven to minister in our behalf. Therefore, the priests, who in representing Christ, could not typify his sinlessness (Heb. 7:28) because all men have sinned, were required to wash before ministering to represent that aspect of Christ's life as our true high priest. This did not teach that the priests sinned every day, but rather it reveals another inadequacy of the Levitical priesthood in representing Christ.

The Holy Place and its Furnishings

"For Christ is not entered into the holy places made with hands, which are the figures of the true; but into the heaven itself, now to appear in the presence of God for us." (Heb. 9:24).

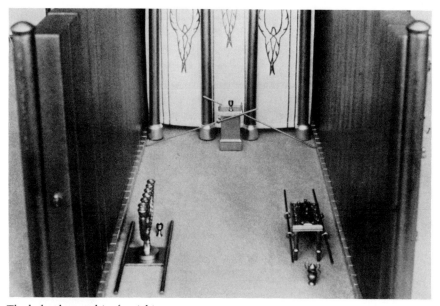

The holy place and its furnishings

Furniture and Accessories

The holy place, the first compartment of the tabernacle proper, contained three items: the candlestick, the table of shewbread, and the incense altar. These items, like the brazen altar in the outer court, represent the various ministries of Christ. At the brazen altar we see men reconciled to God through Christ's death portrayed through animal sacrifices. The brazen altar corresponds to the cross of Calvary. The outer court symbolically represents earth where Christ lived and died for mankind's sin.

Christ's ministry in heaven is typically portrayed by the ministry of the priests in the holy place (Heb. 9:24). Because of this typical significance, the common Israelite could not enter the holy place as he did the outer court. Only the priests were permitted to go into the holy place.

As we seek to understand the tabernacle as the gospel revealed to the Israelites, we need to remember that each furnishing in the holy place is never represented as a type of Christ in itself. As each item represented a ministry of the priest, they also typically represented a ministry of Christ. Here, too, as with the brazen altar, only the most obvious meaning for each item should be emphasized, and that only as it augments the gospel, since the antitype there is lacking any further explanation of their significance. Often the only thing emphasized as significant in the furnishing is its design or dimension. This certainly is not founded upon any antitypical information, and therefore must not be of any significance. We must stress only what God has ordained as significant.

Candlestick

A practical reason for starting with the candlestick (Exod. 25:31–40; 27:20–21; 30:7, 8; 37:17–24; Lev. 24:1–4; Num. 8:1–4) (see chapter 3) and not one of the other two items of the holy place is that, unlike the outer court where there was ample light, the holy place had only the candlestick as a source of light. Light could not penetrate the four-layer covering or the outer veil, and thus another source of light was necessary. The candlestick filled this practical need, since the candlestick was actually a lamp (see chapter 3). Its fuel was pure olive oil and its wicks needed to be trimmed occasionally by tongs provided for this purpose (Exod. 25:38).

Because the candlestick was to burn continually before the Lord, it was necessary for the priests to replenish it with oil and trim its wicks twice daily, morning and evening (Exod. 30:7–8, Lev. 24:3). Only once in Scripture is it recorded that the lamps went out (1 Sam. 3:3, 11–14). This was indicative of the backslidden condition of the priesthood at that time. Also, along with

The Holy Place and its Furnishings

the replenishing of the lamps, the incense was replenished (Exod. 30:7–8), and the daily burnt offering was made (Num. 28:3–4). The importance of this will be considered at the end of this chapter in the ritual of the daily burnt offering.

Since light was the most prominent feature of the candlestick, it is here that we should search for the typical significance of the candlestick in representing the ministry of Christ.

Light is used in scripture as an expression of God's (Luke 2:32; 1 John 1:5) and the Christian's character (Matt. 5:16; Eph. 5:8). Consequently, men who walk contrary to God are said to be in darkness (John 3:19; 8:12; 1 John 1:6). However, all men are said to be lighted by Christ (John 1:9), and thus can be held accountable for their wrong actions (Rom. 2:14–16). Although light is represented in a variety of ways, it is often linked to Christ, who identifies himself as the light of the world (John 8:12). Since the purpose of the candlestick was to produce light and Christ is referred to as the light of the world, this must be the ministry of Christ typified by the candlestick.

In the Old Testament, the means of imparting this light were typically accomplished when the priest poured the pure olive oil into the lamps which produced the illumination. In the New Testament, moral illumination is imparted by Christ's spirit, "Now if any man have not the Spirit of Christ, he is none of his" (Rom. 8:9).

The work of the Holy Spirit in this ministry of Christ can be substantiated in two ways: (1) by the symbolic use of a candlestick or lamps as the Holy Spirit. Revelation 4:5 speaks of seven lamps before the throne of God used symbolically as the Holy Spirit. The same is indicated in Zechariah 4:1–7. (2) oil, the fuel of the candlestick, is related to the work of the Holy Spirit in that it was used as a ceremonial means of consecration in the Old Testament economy, but also identified by Christ as the Holy Spirit, the real means of consecration:

> The Spirit of the Lord is upon me, because he hath anointed me to preach the gospel to the poor; he hath sent me to heal the brokenhearted, to preach deliverance to the captives, and recovering of sight to the blind, to set at liberty them that are bruised. (Luke 4:18)

Although the Holy Spirit plays an important part in this ministry, it is Christ who gives the Holy Spirit to believers. "But when the Comforter is come, whom I will send unto you," (John 15:26). "For if I go not away, the Comforter will not come unto you; but if I depart, I will send him unto you," (John 6:7). These scriptures in particular relate to the outpouring of the Holy Spirit on the Day of Pentecost, but they can be equally applied before this time in a limited sense.

Certainly the Holy Spirit had already been at work in the lives of men before Pentecost, since the Holy Spirit is the agent that produces the new birth (John 3:5–8). John, speaking of the Holy Spirit in John 7:39 as if he had not yet come, must be understood in a relative sense. The Holy Spirit's work and manifestation after Christ's atoning death and the Day of Pentecost is so dramatic that his work before, during the Old Testament period, could be referred to as though he had not yet been given. With the outpouring of Christ's Spirit on Pentecost, all men could be endued with power from on high without measure, whereas the Old Testament saints could only receive the Holy Spirit in measure (Num. 11:16, 17, 25; 2 Kings 2:9–10; Luke 1:15–17).

It is important to note that in this ministry of Christ, unlike at the brazen altar which was open to all, only believers received Christ's spirit. The ministry at the candlestick was only for those who had gone to the brazen altar in godly sorrow for sin, or who go to Christ today. And so it is that the spirit of Christ is only given to the true believer: Jesus speaking of the Holy Spirit said "Whom the world cannot receive" (John 14:17).

The work of the spirit of Christ illuminating the minds of the saints can be compared to the natural world's need of sunlight. Like light, he is absolutely essential for life, because it is only through the Holy Spirit that man can receive life from God:

> But as it is written, Eye hath not seen, nor ear heard, neither have entered into the heart of man, the things which God hath prepared for them that love him. But God hath revealed them unto us by his Spirit: for the Spirit searcheth all things, yea, the deep things of God. For what man knoweth the things of a man, save the spirit of man which is in him even so the things of God knoweth no man, but the Spirit of God. Now we have received, not the spirit of the world, but the spirit which is of God; that we might know the things that are freely given to us of God. Which things also we

speak, not in the words which man's wisdom teacheth, but which the Holy Ghost teacheth; comparing spiritual things with spiritual. But the natural man receiveth not the things of the Spirit of God: for they are foolishness unto him: neither can he know them, because they are spiritually discerned. But he that is spiritual judgeth all things, yet he himself is judged of no man. For who hath known the mind of the Lord, that he may instruct him? But we have the mind of Christ (1 Cor. 2:9–16).

So Christ sends the spirit of truth to the believers to teach them, to guide them into all truth, and to testify of and glorify Christ (John 14:26; 15:26; 16:13, 14). Without this ministry of Christ, the saint would soon wither as a plant without sunlight.

Table of Shewbread

The table of shewbread (Exod. 25:23–30; 37:10–16; Lev. 24:5–9) (see chapter 3) was on the north side of the holy place, opposite the candlestick.

The significance of the table of shewbread, like all the furnishings, is not found in the item itself, but rather with what was on it. On the table of shewbread were twelve loaves of bread called shewbread or, more literally, bread of my face, since they were always before the Lord, shewbread being the vehicle through which God could be seen as typified by Christ (John 4:9).

Each unleavened loaf was made of $2/10$ deal of fine flour, which is equivalent to about a gallon. The loaves were flat and measured approximately eighteen inches in diameter, and together weighed approximately ninety pounds. These twelve loaves were probably enough to last the whole week, since only the officiating priest could eat them. They could only be eaten in the outer court. New loaves were exchanged each sabbath.

Although the shewbread was meant for only the priests, Ahimelech, the priest in Nob, gave some to David and his men, since it was the only food available (1 Sam. 21:1–6). These were the loaves already taken from the table for the priest, and not those still on the table. In reference to this incident, Jesus did not consider it sinful when David and his men ate of the shewbread (Matt. 12:2–4, Mark 2:25, 26; Luke 6:2–4). The reason is because Ahimelech had inquired of the Lord, who gave permission in this case (1 Sam. 22:10).

The amount of oil used in making the shewbread, if any, is not stated. If oil was used, it was probably the amount used in other meat offerings of this size, or ⅓ hin or 2 quarts (Num. 15:6). As in other meat offerings, frankincense was the only part of the shewbread burned on the brazen altar.

Because the shewbread was actually a meat offering, it is believed that the loaves were made without leaven as with the regular meat offerings, to comply with the prohibition against burning leaven on the brazen altar. Since the shewbread was eaten by the priests and not burned on the brazen altar, it did not necessarily have to be free of leaven. If, however, leaven was used, it probably would have been mentioned specifically as in the feast of Pentecost (Lev. 23:17).

For the Israelite, the significance of the shewbread is found in that it was a meat offering (see Meat Offering, page 142). The continual meat offering of the shewbread was not offered because the Israelites thought God needed food. It served rather as a constant reminder to God of their reliance on him to meet their needs. At the same time, it stood as a reminder to them that they must depend on God for their needs: thus, twelve loaves apparently represented each tribe.

Food, being man's most frequent need, served well as a representation of God as provider. This should have been a great encouragement to the Israelites who had left the bountiful land of Egypt for a desert where the basic necessities of life were lacking. Even though God provided for them, they complained and wanted to return to Egypt (Num. 1:4–6; 14:1–4). Thus, after forty wasted years in the desert, Moses revealed that the necessity for the provision of manna was to teach them that man does not live by bread alone but by every word that proceedeth out of the mouth of the Lord (Deut. 8:2–6).

God's provision of manna for forty years in the wilderness was a practical demonstration to the nation of what the shewbread represented: that God does provide for physical needs. Unfortunately, its more important lesson of reliance on God for eternal security by obedience to his word was not learned by that first generation of Israelites (Exod. 16:32–34; Num. 21:5). New Testament saints must learn the same lesson.

In reference to our spiritual needs, Jesus Christ is identified as the bread of life (John 6:48), which is of infinitely greater value than temporal needs (Matt. 16:26). As the bread of life, Jesus is saying to us, "I can provide for you not just for forty years as the manna did for the Israelites in the wilderness, but if you eat of me you will live forever" (John 6:51). This comes by our emulation of his life, and by faith in his atoning death, the only means for the removal of sin. Christ said he would give his flesh for the life of the world. Thus, as bread provides for man's physical needs, Christ's atoning death provides for man's spiritual needs. The priests, by eating the shewbread every sabbath, typified Jesus' provision of our spiritual needs.

This same principle (a priest representing Christ) is seen in the animal sacrifices, after which a priest ate a portion of an offering as he ministered, so that together both he and the offering could fully typify Christ as both priest and sacrifice.

The spirit of Christ is also seen in his ministry at the table of shewbread in that the shewbread was not visible in the sanctuary except by the light from the candlestick, teaching that the saint of God must always walk in the illuminating light of the Holy Spirit in order to have Christ revealed as the living bread from heaven. It is only by the ministry of Christ's spirit that we can learn that man does not live by bread alone but by every word that proceedeth out of the mouth of the Lord (Deut. 8:3).

In our growth as Christians we have two choices as the Holy Spirit continually reveals Christ as the bread of life: we can be offended at what he says, and go back as some of his disciples did (John 6:61, 66), or we can, like the faithful twelve, say: "to whom shall we go? thou hast the words of eternal life. And we believe and are sure that thou art that Christ, the son of the living God" (John 6:68, 69).

Altar of Incense

We now come to the last furnishing of the holy place, the altar of incense (Exod. 30:1–10; 37:25–28), which was located at the west end of the sanctuary before the inner veil. This position is significant since it was located nearest the ark within the holy of holies (see chapter 3).

The purpose of this item was, as its name suggests, the place for burning incense. Here the priests would twice daily burn sweet incense. This was done at the same time the oil in the candlestick was replenished (Exod. 30:7–8) and the daily burnt offering was made (Num. 28:3, 4). Although the priests had a variety of duties to perform, their work at the incense altar characterized their overall work (Deut. 33:10; 1 Sam. 2:28; 2 Chron. 29:11). This indicates the altar's importance.

"And Aaron was separated, that he should sanctify the most holy things, he and his sons for ever, to burn incense before the LORD, to minister unto him, and to bless in his name for ever," 1 Chron. 23:13. Thus, they only were sanctioned as ministers at the altar of incense. Therefore, when Korah led 250 princes in seeking the priesthood (Num. 16:10), and took censers for burning incense, and stood before the Lord to see if they could come near to him as priests, they were promptly judged (Num. 16:35). It is fitting that their censers were used to make a covering for the brazen altar as a memorial that only Aaron and his sons could offer incense before the Lord (Num. 16:39, 40). Many years later, King Uzziah did not heed the warning of this incident and went into the temple and offered incense. He was immediately struck with leprosy. That only Aaron and his sons should come before the Lord was not an empty threat.

The most severe judgment in association with the incense altar did not come from without the priesthood, but within. Nadab and Abihu, Aaron's sons, were both consumed by a fire from the Lord when they went into the sanctuary with incense (Lev. 10:1–2). The only reason given for this retribution was that they used fire from other than the brazen altar, called strange fire (Lev. 10:1; Num. 3:4). Leviticus 10:9 indicates that their impudence was due to drunkenness, while the reference to their death is given with the instructions for the ritual of the Day of Atonement. This may suggest that they went into the holy of holies (Lev. 16:1–2).

Although there is no mention of a specific vessel for the burning of incense, we know that there was a censer because of its mention in the ritual of the Day of Atonement (Lev. 16:12–13) and from mention of a golden censer in Hebrews 9:4. Though the writer of the Book of Hebrews does not specifically say that the golden censer was from the incense altar, he does state that it was in the holy of holies before the ark, which corresponds to the ritual of the Day of Atonement when sweet incense was burned before the ark. On the Day of Atonement, instead of moving the incense altar into the holy of holies, only the censer in which the sweet incense was burned was taken in. Thus, there is no mention of the incense altar itself. This illustrates that it was not the item which was important but what was on it. The brazen altar without an offering would have no efficacy, the candlestick without oil would be useless, the table of shewbread without bread would illustrate nothing, and likewise, the incense altar without incense would be meaningless as well.

Unlike the brazen altar, it was expressly forbidden to offer "strange" incense (incense not made according to divine instructions), burnt sacrifices, meat or drink offerings on the incense altar (Exod. 30:9). Like the brazen altar, however, it was a means of access to God. This is important in determining the ministry of Christ portrayed at the incense altar.

The means of access portrayed here can be seen by the symbolic use of incense as prayer:

"Let my prayer be set forth before thee as incense" (Ps. 141:2).
"And golden vials full of odours, which are the prayers of saints" (Rev. 5:8).
"And another angel came and stood at the altar, having a golden censer; and there was given unto him much incense, that he should offer it with the prayers of all saints upon the golden altar which was before the throne. And the smoke of the incense, which came with the prayers of the saints, ascended up before God out of the angel's hand" (Rev. 8:3, 4).

Jewish tradition teaches that the priests prayed at the incense altar and from Luke 1:8-10, it seems to have become a custom also for the people to pray at the time of offering incense.

Because of the fact that altars represent access to God (the brazen altar through sacrifice and the incense altar through prayer), we can conclude that the incense altar represents the intercessory ministry of Christ. Access to God taught at the brazen altar stemmed from the separation sin brought. This separation was fully breached by Christ's expiatory death. The access available at the incense altar through prayer was not limited to only those who had gone to the brazen altar for atonement, but was actually effectual for all the Hebrews on a continual basis.

Despite the priests' twice daily intercession on behalf of the nation at the incense altar, their intercessory prayers were only a temporary and inadequate representation of Christ's intercessory ministry. Scriptural passages which support the efficacy of Christ's intercessory ministry include:

> "And he bare the sin of many, and made intercession for the transgressors" (Isa. 53:12).
> "He ever liveth to make intercession for them" (Heb. 7:25).
> "Who is even at the right hand of God, who also maketh intercession for us" (Rom. 8:34).
> "And if any man sin, we have an advocate with the Father, Jesus Christ the righteous: And he is the propitiation for our sins: and not for ours only, but also for the sins of the whole world" (1 John 2:1–2).

The saints can learn an important lesson from the priests' ministry at the incense altar. With the incense altar standing just before the inner veil, which separated the holy place from the holy of holies, the priests ministered as close as they could come to the presence of God. This is equally true of the saints when they pray. We can come no closer to the presence of God than when we intercede in prayer.

The Ritual of the Daily Burnt Offering

So far we have only viewed each furnishing individually to discover the particular ministry it portrayed. Now, however, we need to consider them as they function together. If we study them only individually, we will have a myopic picture of the ministries of Christ. Viewed corporately, however, we see the harmonious relationship of each to the other as well as their dependence on one another. Only by understanding their integral relationship can we gain a proper understanding of Christ's total work. This can be seen best through the ritual of the daily burnt offering.

It is interesting to see how so many seemingly unrelated activities of the priest's work were associated with the same time of day, morning and evening. There was the daily burnt offering (Num. 28:3–4), the replenishing of oil for the candlestick (Lev. 24:3), the burning of incense at the incense altar (Exod. 30:7–8), and the removal of the ashes from the brazen altar to a clean place outside of the camp (Lev. 6:8–12). These activities involved every furnishing of the outer court and the holy place twice daily. The responsibility for these tasks belonged to the priests, whose activities reveal a clear picture of their significance.

The Holy Place and its Furnishings

Several priests were involved with performing these duties. There were three areas of work: at the holy place, at the brazen altar, and outside the camp where the ashes were dumped. This would necessitate at least three priests (the number left after the death of Nadab and Abihu) if the work in these areas was to be done simultaneously. If not simultaneous, the probable order would have been carrying the ashes outside the camp, making the offerings, followed by ministering in the holy place. Our description will follow this order.

The removal of the ashes from the brazen altar was not an insignificant chore, at least not typically. The wood used to burn the evening burnt offering, and any other offerings afterwards, was only ashes in the ash pans under the grate by morning. A priest would remove these pans from under the altar and then change into other garments before carrying them out to the ash pile outside the camp (Lev. 6:11). The Levites probably did the actual transporting of the ash pans. Although the ashes were taken outside the camp, this removal was not insignificant (Heb. 13:11–12). This was evidence of God's satisfaction with the animal offered. This was also the site where the sin offerings for the high priest and congregation were taken to be burnt (Lev. 4:12, 21), which is typical of Christ who was taken outside the gates of Jerusalem to suffer the penalty of sin. The changing of the priest's clothes at this time may represent Christ in his humanity and not his heavenly glory, because he went to the cross not as a priest but as a sacrifice which made his mediatory work efficacious.

To further express the efficacy of the priests' ministry, many of their works were called perpetual or continual, both the same Hebrew word. The daily burnt offering, except for the one in Numbers 29:6, was called the continual burnt offering, the fire on the brazen altar was perpetual for it was never to go out (Lev. 6:13), the candlestick was to burn continually (Lev. 24:2), the shewbread was called continual bread (Num. 4:7) because it was always before the Lord, and the incense was to burn perpetually (Exod. 30:8). This is indicative of their importance in the priests' ministry typifying Christ's work which is indeed perpetual.

The morning daily burnt offering consisted of a lamb along with its meat and drink offering. The burnt offering was the only offering made on a daily basis (Exod. 29:38–42), the others being made only as the need arose. Although the meat and drink offerings accompanied the daily burnt offering, it was not offered to denote the national aspect of the continual consecration to God, but rather, it was offered to denote the priestly aspect of their continual consecration to God and thus typified Christ's continual consecration. The burnt offering, which typified consecration, could best typify Christ's complete and total surrender to God for us: thus, all his ministries were described as continual. The sin offering was not offered daily because Christ died only once.

For the morning daily burnt offering, the priest would take an unblemished lamb to the north side of the altar, and there lay his hands on its head while making a confession of continual service and dedication to God. Then, he would cut its throat and catch its blood in a brazen bowl. After washing at the laver (A), he would sprinkle the blood on the brazen altar (B). Next, he would butcher the animal, keeping the skin for himself. The head and fat were laid on the fire of the brazen altar, but the legs and inwards were first washed at the laver as were the priest's hands and feet before he took them to the brazen altar. The meat and drink offerings were then offered and salt was strewn over all of the sacrifices. If Leviticus 6:23 applies to any meat offering for a priest and not just those at the time of the anointing of a new high priest, then the whole meat offering was burnt and not just a small portion.

The priest would then take a brass censer full of coals from the brazen altar to the laver to wash again. Then he would enter the holy place (C). Since the candlestick had its own golden censer, the coals were probably transferred to it. He would then trim the wicks and replenish the oil of the candlestick, relighting each lamp with the coals from the brazen altar (D). He next placed incense in the censer on top of the incense altar. Since the only place spoons, the vessels for holding the incense, are mentioned is at the table of shewbread (E), the priest would stop there to get the sweet incense and light it with the coals from the brazen altar (F).

These morning and evening priestly duties each beautifully portray the continual ministry of Christ as our true priest. The continual burnt offering represents Christ's complete and continual service to God for us. In the meat offering and its drink offering we see Christ in his service to man. The fire consumed the offering, changing it to smoke and ashes. Ashes were the evidence

The Holy Place and its Furnishings

A

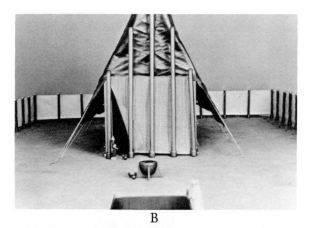

B

C

The ritual of the burnt offering

174   Panoramic View of the Tabernacle

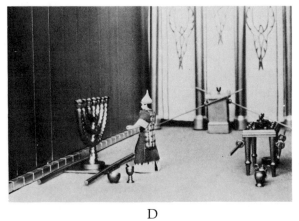

D

E

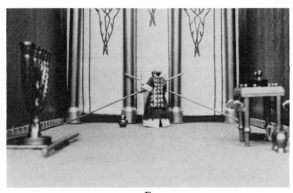

F

The ritual of the daily burnt offering

of the finished work, and the smoke was a witness of God's satisfaction with Christ, it being called a sweet savour. The washing at the laver was necessary to portray Christ's sinlessness, which made it possible for him to ascend to heaven. His heavenly ministries portrayed in the holy place by its three furnishings were all linked to the offerings at the brazen altar. It was his vicarious life and death portrayed in the sacrifices at the brazen altar that rendered his other ministries efficacious for the believer. Thus, the coals were taken from the brazen altar into the holy place to light the candlestick and incense.

We see, therefore, that it was only those who went to the brazen altar in acknowledgment of God's provision who received the benefits of the priests' ministries in the holy place. Likewise today, we must go to Calvary before we can receive Christ as our advocate, as well as bountiful provisions, promises, and blessings that a loving God is willing to bestow on his people.

8 The Holy of Holies and the Ark

"Having therefore, brethren, boldness to enter into the holiest by the blood of Jesus" (Heb. 10:19).

The high priest at the ark in the holy of holies

The holy of holies, the second compartment of the sanctuary, was separated from the holy place by the inner veil. Entrance into it was allowed only once a year on the Day of Atonement, and was restricted to the high priest himself. This limited access is indicative of the importance of its furnishings: the ark and mercy seat. Usually the two are referred to as the ark, although the mercy seat is a distinct and separate item. This physical link will be important later in considering their typical significance.

The absence of any figures of God on the ark is a noticeable feature, since heathens often placed figures of their deity on their arks. This, along with the second commandment, discouraged idol making. Although it is true no one but the high priest ever saw the ark uncovered, its features were probably well known from comments by the priests as well as the written word.

Charge of the ark was given to the Kohathites, who were instructed to wait until it was properly covered by the priests before they were called to move it. Ordinarily, the place of the ark during a journey appears to have been in the middle of the nation, since this was the location of the Kohathites (Num. 10:21). Other scriptural passages state that the ark always led the way during the nation's journeying, specifically the first movement of the nation from Mount Sinai (Num. 10:33–36), and the passage across the Jordan River (Josh. 3:3; 4:18); but this may be because these were hallmarks during the Israelites' sojourn. Scripture also teaches that the ark was taken from the holy of holies on special occasions or battles, such as the battle against the Midianites (Num. 31:6–7), the fall of Jericho (Josh. 6:4–13), at the Mount of Blessing and Cursing (Josh. 8:33), and the war with the Philistines (1 Sam. 4:3–6). Numbers 14:44 and 1 Samuel 14:18 also suggest that the ark was taken along on other important occasions.

When God gave instructions concerning the ark, he said it was to contain what he would give (Exod. 25:16). From Hebrews 9:4, we learn there were three items in the ark: the two tablets of the covenant, a golden pot of manna, and Aaron's rod that budded. The first items placed into the ark were the two covenant tablets. Moses brought the second set of tablets down from Mt. Sinai on his eighth and last descent. They were not placed in the ark until seven months later, after the tabernacle and ark were constructed (Exod. 34:29; 40:20). Deuteronomy 10:1–5 states that Moses put this second set of covenant tablets in an ark that he made immediately on his descent. Obviously, Moses did make an ark before he ascended Mount Sinai to receive the tablets and this ark served as a temporary container until they were placed in the ark Bezaleel (Exod. 37:1) constructed. The golden pot of manna was commanded to be placed in the ark sometime before the nation's arrival at Mount Sinai (Exod. 16:33), but could not have been done for at least another ten months, probably at the same time the tablets were put there. The manna was no doubt preserved by divine intervention since manna would normally decay in one day (Exod. 16:20). The rod of Aaron was placed in the ark sometime during the wilderness wanderings, probably during their first year. Some people believe the book of the law was also kept in the ark. Whether this is in reference to the entire Pentateuch or just the Book of Deuteronomy is not certain; in either case, it was only placed next to the ark (Deut. 31:26). At the time the ark was brought into Solomon's temple, only the two tablets of the covenant remained. (2 Chron. 5:10). There is no record of when the golden pot of manna and Aaron's rod were removed, but their removal probably occurred when the ark was captured by the Philistines.

The three items in the ark were a testimony of God's providing providence (see photo 23), as well as the nation's chronic rebellion. The two covenant tablets were called the tablets of testimony (Exod. 34:29) because in them were embodied all the other laws which were given for the nation's well-being (Deut. 10:13). There was no nation on earth which had such glorious laws (Deut. 4:8; Ps. 147:19–20), but they also witnessed against the nation for their many deliberate transgressions of the law (Deut. 31:26). The golden pot of manna was a testimony of God's provision of food in the barren wilderness (Exod. 16:32), but it also tested the nation's obedience (Exod. 16:4, 20, 27–28; Num. 21:5). Aaron's rod, although it was a memorial of God's choice of the Aaronic priesthood, stood as a reminder of the nation's rebellion at this choice (Num. 16, 17).

In considering the ark as a type, there are some noticeable differences from what we find concerning the other furnishings. There was the special chamber, the holy of holies, which housed the ark. This was the most sacred part of the tabernacle. However, the holy of holies derived its importance from the presence of the ark. There were no daily, weekly, or even monthly activities associated with the ark. The high priest could enter into the holy of holies once each year on the Day of Atonement, which was the only ritual that pertained to the ark. The high priest's function on this day was quite different from his ministries at the other furnishings. At the brazen altar there were the perpetual fire and sacrifices to attend to, there was his washing at the laver, there was the need to replenish the oil of the candlestick, the eating of bread at the table of shewbread and the incense burning at the incense altar, all of which necessitated the priest's daily attention.

At the ark, however, there was nothing that required his presence. When the high priest went before the ark, it was not in the sense of ministering as it was at the other furnishings, although he brought in the blood of the sin offering and the incense, the evidence of his ministry at the other items.

Although the ark and mercy seat are surely typical, as are the other items, there is little explanation of their significance. With the other furnishings, because the priests ministered at each of them, we understand them as representing the various ministries of Christ. With the ark, because of its isolation and lack of similarity to the other furnitures, its typology is only implied. Hebrews 9:24 states that when Christ ascended to heaven (holy place) it was to appear in the presence of God. Since, so far, all salient aspects of the gospel are represented in the tabernacle except God, and because the ark is the only furniture not a type of Christ's ministries, we can conclude from Hebrews 9:24 that it represents God the Father.

This is verified by Israeli history, which points to the ark as being synonymous with God. For this reason, the ark led the way in the wilderness wanderings and was taken into battle often. When Israel brought the ark into the camp after their defeat by the Philistines, their shouts were understood by the Philistines to mean that the ark was with them. The Philistines' reply was "God is come into the camp" (1 Sam. 4:7–8). Later, after the ark was captured by the Philistines, Phinehas' wife gave birth and named the child Ichabod, meaning the glory is departed from Israel (1 Sam. 4:22). When Solomon dedicated the temple, he said the temple which he had made could not contain God (1 Kings 8:27; 2 Chron. 6:18). Which part of the temple did he consider as representing God? Surely it was the ark, the only item from the tabernacle to be placed in Solomon's temple.

The mercy seat also, like the ark, was thought of as representing God (1 Sam. 4:4; Ps. 80:1; 99:1). From between the two cherubim on the mercy seat God spoke to the nation through the high priest (Exod. 25:22; 30:6; Lev. 16:2; Num. 7:89). The mercy seat is often taught to be a type of Jesus Christ because the word *propitiation* in Romans 3:25 is the word translated *mercy seat* in Hebrews 9:5. The difficulty with thinking of Christ as the antitype of the mercy seat is that this would make the high priest, who typifies Christ, as presenting the blood of the sacrifice, to himself.

The ark and mercy seat teach two fundamental aspects of God's character. Here man approached God as a sinner. He had broken God's laws and came to him in an attitude of repentance. No matter how deep his contrition, it could not modify what he had done. The law still condemned. Repentance alone cannot satisfy the damage to God's authority and law. For God to wisely extend his mercy, the sinner had to bring an offering, which typified Christ, whose vicarious death did satisfy God and made possible his mercy to those who came with true sorrow for their sins. Thus, we see two attributes of God: his justice in his regard to honoring his law, and his mercy in his disposition to pardon those who broke the law. Therefore, the ark, which contained the law, represented God's justice while the mercy seat, where the blood was applied, represented pardon or his attribute of mercy.

To properly understand the ark's typical importance, as well as the Day of Atonement which centers around the ark, we must understand the relationship of these two attributes of God. We must also view them as they relate to a criminal, since in the gospel this is our condition when we come before God. As such, justice would be the execution of the penalty of the law and mercy a disposition to forgive those who deserve punishment. Justice and mercy in relation to crime are diametrically opposed to one another; justice would punish while mercy would forgive. But, since both are attributes of God, they cannot be used in opposition to one another. The mercy of God never abolished his moral law to harmonize justice and mercy. This belief stems from references to the ceremonial laws, which typified Christ and the gospel, and the penalty of the law, which was satisfied in Christ's atoning death.

All men are still obligated to keep God's moral laws because they can never be abolished (Matt. 5:17, 18). There can be no justice without law, and if God could abolish his law, there would be no need to preach a gospel which releases man from the law's penalty. What God actually did was annex the gospel to his law, the real means of bringing harmony to justice and mercy and the only remedy for mankind's transgressions. To do away with the moral law would, in essence, abolish the gospel because it derived all its value from the fact that it offers pardon to those who have broken the law. The atonement was the means used to accomplish this. It is this grand theme that is taught in the ritual of the

Day of Atonement, which typifies the efficacy of Christ's "one" sacrifice. This is the reason for the limited usage of the ark and the mercy seat on only one day each year.

Since moral beings require laws for their happiness and well-being, the means of reconciliation of justice and mercy must be as effective as if the penalty on the transgressors was inflicted. The vicarious and atoning death of Christ answers all the purposes which the execution of the law would have answered. In addition to its being a pardon, atonement was used by God to impress on mankind the perfection of his laws and their sanctions for the welfare of all moral beings. The law's penalty reveals God's intense hatred of sin, and acts as a necessary means to prevent lawlessness. The law itself is the moral scale by which we must graduate our actions. The atonement and the penalty of the law were to act as a motive for obedience. The atonement reveals the regard God has for his law; otherwise, he would never have gone to such lengths to uphold it.

If God would have pardoned man without atonement, he would have shown no regard for his law and, instead of preventing sin, encouraged it. Thus, Christ's suffering and humiliating death teaches the intense hatred God has of sin, as well as revealing his tremendous love to mankind. The atonement would thus act as a greater deterrent to sin and a greater inducement to live a holy life than the execution of the law's penalty. The atonement renders honor to God's law, to his character, and his kingdom.

In regard to pardon, which can come only through the atonement, God's thoughts and ways are far above ours (Isa. 55:7–9). How glorious his ways are! Even the angelic beings are amazed by the manifold wisdom of God as expressed in the atonement. They desire to look into the gospel because, under their circumstances (spirit beings with a greater knowledge of God) an atonement was not wise for certain angels who rebelled against God. Thus, all of God's creation benefits from Christ's atonement, and receives a greater knowledge of God than otherwise would have been possible; thus, the cherubim are over the mercy seat, on the inner veil, and the inner coverings of the tabernacle.

The Ritual of the Day of Atonement

On a corporate and individual level, hundreds of sacrifices were offered by Israel yearly. These offerings appropriated their efficacy from what was typically taught on the Day of Atonement. The many offerings of Israel could not typically teach that Christ would come once to die for the sins of the world. They were only the means of appropriating by faith the effect of Christ's one sacrifice; therefore, there was a need to express this typically. The Day of Atonement satisfies this need.

The Day of Atonement is described in three separate passages of scripture. In Leviticus 16, we have the detailed instructions for the high priest's duties pertaining to its special sin offering; Leviticus 23:26–32 describes the holy convocation when they were to afflict their souls and Numbers 29:7–11 gives information concerning the other offerings offered on this day. It should be noted that much of Hebrews 9 is atypical of the Day of Atonement. All further verses, unless stated otherwise, are taken from Leviticus 16.

The Day of Atonement was observed during the fall after the crops were harvested. Many people would be coming to the tabernacle for the feast of trumpets on the first day of the Hebrew seventh month, or later to the feast of tabernacles, on the fifteenth day when all males were required to attend. The Day of Atonement was observed on the tenth day between these two feasts. These dates correspond roughly to the Julian September and October. It was the most sacred day of the year and the only day on which the Israelites were commanded to afflict their souls by fasting. This was in solemn preparation for the special sin offerings being offered for the nation's sins (vv. 29–30). The priests' preparation for making the special offerings on this day, like the peoples', were different than usual (for the other offerings on the Day of Atonement, see page 156). Though the priests always washed their hands and feet at the laver before ministering at the brazen altar or in the sanctuary, on this day, due to the solemnity of the event, the high priest washed his whole body (v. 4). Even his attire was special. He did not wear the breastplate, ephod or robe of the ephod. He wore only the linen coat, linen girdle, linen breeches, and the mitre, all of which were called the holy garments. Thus, he was dressed all in white (v. 4). White clothing in scripture is associated with holy angels and holy saints (Ezek. 9:2; Matt. 28:3; Mark 16:5; John 20:12; Rev. 19:7–8). How fitting that the high priest, who mediated and offered sacrifices on behalf of the nations, should wear white, symbolizing the purity and righteousness of Christ, our real mediator and true sacrifice.

A

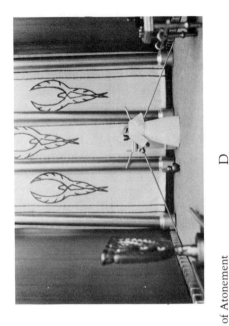

B

C

D

The Ritual of the Day of Atonement

E

F

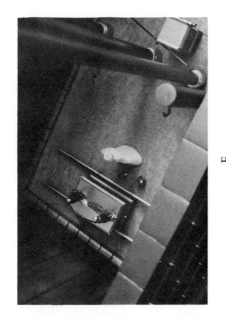

G

H

The Ritual of the Day of Atonement

The high priest would then make ready the animals for the offering. For the congregation, two goats were used for their sin offering and one ram for their burnt offering. The high priest would cast lots, probably with the urim and thummim, to determine which goat would be offered on the brazen altar and which released as a scapegoat (A). He then laid his hands on the bullock for his own sin offering, confessing his sin (B). He killed the bullock, catching its blood in a bowl. After washing at the laver (C), he proceeded into the sanctuary where he took up the golden censer, which was full of coals, from the brazen altar, and also picked up a handful of sweet incense (D).

He then went into the holy of holies, and placed the golden censer before the mercy seat, and added the incense to cause a cloud of smoke to fill the room (E). Leviticus states that the high priest would die if he failed to burn the incense so that the cloud covered the mercy seat (v. 13). This may be explained by the fact that man cannot look on the full glory of God (Exod. 33:20–23; 1 Tim. 6:16). God often veils himself in a cloud as he did during Moses' sixth ascent of Mount Sinai (Exod. 24:15–18); on Moses' eighth ascent to get the second set of covenant tablets (Exod. 34:5); when the tabernacle was first set up (Exod. 40:34–38); at the dedication of Solomon's temple (1 Kings 8:10–11, 2 Chron. 5:13–14), and on the Day of Atonement (Lev. 16:2). Thus, because the ark was typical of God, it was necessary to veil it in a cloud, too.

This does not abrogate the typical meaning of the incense as the intercessory work of Christ on behalf of mankind. Christ's intercessory ministry is seen here through the burning incense, which speaks of his pleading on our behalf. Because of his vicarious death, all who come in repentance may receive a pardon for sins. Thus, we see how the atonement began with Christ's intercession.

Next, the high priest took the blood from his own sin offering, and sprinkled it seven times before and on the mercy seat before going to the outer court where he killed the sacrificial goat (F). He brought its blood into the holy of holies and sprinkled it as he did with the blood of his own sacrifices (G). It was this special application of blood on the mercy seat that speaks of the sacrifice at the altar, typifying Christ's sacrifice at Calvary, which made it possible for God's mercy to be extended to mankind. The reason

The Holy of Holies and the Ark   187

the blood had to be brought into the holy of holies before the ark, and not just to the brazen altar, was to teach that Christ's atoning death could be efficacious only as it regarded God the Father.

As he left the holy of holies, the high priest would make atonement for the holy place. This was accomplished by sprinkling blood, possibly on the veil, as done in the sin offering for the high priest, and on the horns of the incense altar to comply with Exodus 30:10. The blood was also put on the horns of the brazen altar and sprinkled on the altar itself to make atonement (v. 18). This was done because of the uncleanliness of the people (vv. 16, 19).

All of the activity of the high priest to this point was done without the usual assistance of the other priests (v. 17). No other person, priest or Levite, was allowed in the tabernacle until atonement was made. Christ in his work as expiator and mediator needed no assistance, so the high priest, in typifying this, was not assisted on this day, "For there is one God and one mediator between God and man, the man Christ Jesus" (1 Tim. 2:5).

The priest then took the second goat of the sin offering, laid his hands on its head and confessed the sins of the nation. This goat was then led to an uninhabited area and released, symbolizing its bearing of their iniquities (H).

Only on the Day of Atonement was there ever offered more than one animal for a sin offering. Single animal offerings for sin was a distinct characteristic of the sin offering, but on this day two animals constituted one offering. The reason for this is that it would be physically impossible for one animal to typically express all that needed to be set forth. Even tradition complied with this in that it is said that both animals chosen were of the same size, color and value. The purpose of the second goat, which was called the scapegoat, or goat of departure, was typically to teach the resurrection of Christ.

Other meanings have been applied to the scapegoat, but they are not consistent with the typical teaching of the Day of Atonement. The first goat was offered on the brazen altar, because without shedding of blood there could be no remissions of sin, typifying Christ's death on Calvary. However, the thing that made Christ's death efficacious was his resurrection: thus, the need for the second goat. Paul said that "if Christ be not raised your faith is in vain; ye are yet in your sins" (1 Cor. 15:17). It was the resurrection that proved Christ was not subject to death because of his sinlessness, which also qualified him to be a vicarious sacrifice for mankind. The second goat, spared from death, was typical of the resurrection.

Next, the high priest washed his whole body at the laver and changed into his other garments of "glory and beauty." Two rams for a burnt offering were then offered, and the fat of the bullock and goat of the sin offerings were burned on the brazen altar. The remains of the bullock and goat of the sin offerings were carried outside the camp and burned. This completed the ceremony of the Day of Atonement and typically taught that Christ suffered outside the gates of Jerusalem (Heb. 13:11–12). The Israelites who led the goat into the wilderness, and carried the sin offering outside the camp were to wash themselves and their clothing before returning to the camp. These ceremonial washings and those of the high priest must have impressed the people with the pervading evilness of sin, even on those who are only ceremonially affected by it.

Although the Day of Atonement expressed the removal of the sins of the nation, ironically there was never any true efficacy in those sacrifices, "for it is not possible that blood of bulls and of goats should take away sins" (Heb. 10:4). There was, however, lasting efficacy in what they typified. Hidden within the inner veil of the tabernacle, God beautifully typified when consummate atonement would be realized. Hebrews 10:20 says "By a new and living way, which he hath consecrated for us, through the veil, that is to say, his flesh." It would not be until Christ, having the flesh of men and tempted like men, and yet without sin, came and offered his body and the shedding of his blood to satisfy the just demand of God for sin that the human race could be truly reconciled to God. Upon Christ's death the veil of Herod's temple in Jerusalem, which corresponded to the inner veil of the tabernacle, was torn from top to bottom the moment Christ said, "It is finished" (John 19:30; Matt. 27:48–51), indicating that God's demand for justice was finally satisfied. The high priest could never make such a statement as "it is finished." His work was never finished; "But this man after he had offered one sacrifice for sins for ever, sat down on the right hand of God" (Heb. 10:12).

It is sometimes taught that the veil separated the Old Testament saints from God and that only the New Testament saints have the privilege of going into God's presence. This is not true; the Old Testament saints had access to God, but it had to be through a priest and an animal sacrifice. Our access is different in that Christ, our high priest and sacrifice, is seated at the right hand of God where we can take our petitions directly without a human mediator. This is that "new and living way" (Heb. 10:20).

Another important event that occurred on the Day of Atonement was the blowing of the trumpets to announce the year of Jubilee which occurred every fifty years. This was to announce a full release of slaves, debts, and the restoration of all lands to their owners. Upon the authority of Christ and Old Testament prophecy, we know this typifies the effect of Christ's atoning death (Isa. 61:1–2; Luke 4:18–21). How fitting that this should augment the teaching of the Day of Atonement, because through Christ we, too, can be delivered from sin and its power, and restored to God. Though the Jubilee lasted for only a year in the Old Testament economy, it denotes an age for us: "Now is the accepted time; behold, now is the day of salvation" (2 Cor. 6:2).

Bibliography

Carter, John. *God's Tabernacle in the Wilderness and its Principal Offerings* (Springfield, Mo.: Gospel Publishing House, 2nd ed., 1970).

Cornwall, Judson. *Let Us Draw Near* (Plainfield, N.J.: Logos International, 1977).

Epp, Theodore H. *Portraits of Christ in the Tabernacle* (Lincoln, Neb.: Back to the Bible, 1976).

Habershon, Ada R., *Outline Studies of the Tabernacle* (Grand Rapids: Kregel Publications, 2nd ed., 1977).

Laity, Edward, Lt. Colonel (R). *Tabernacle Types and Teachings* (Atlanta: Southern territory U.S.A.: The Salvation Army, 1973).

Jukes, Andrew. *The Law of the Offerings* (Grand Rapids: Kregel Publications, 2nd, ed., Paperback, 1980).

Kiene, Paul F. *The Tabernacle of God in the Wilderness of Sinai* (Grand Rapids: Zondervan Publishing House, 1977).

Olford, Stephen F. *The Tabernacle: Camping with God* (Neptune, N.J.: Loizeaux Brothers, 1971).

Ridout, Samuel. *Lectures on the Tabernacle* (Neptune, N.J.: Loizeaux Brothers, first ed., 1914).

Slemming, Charles W. *Made According to Pattern* (Fort Washington, Pa.: Christian Literature Crusade, first Amer. ed., 1971).

_____ *Thus Shalt Thou Serve* (Fort Washington, Pa.: Christian Literature Crusade, first Amer. ed., 1974).

Soltau, Henry W. *The Holy Vessels and Furniture of the Tabernacle* (Grand Rapids: Kregel Publications, 1975).

Zehr, Paul M. *God Dwells with His People* (Scottdale, Pa.: Herald Press, 1981).

Index

Aaron, 75, 168, *See* chapter 4
Abel, 19
Abihu, 168
Acacia tree, 46, *See* shittim wood
Aholiab, 42, 48
Altar, brazen, 53, 54, 118-120, 124; incense, 48, 66, 167-170
Animals, a type, 108, 109; *See* offerings
Anointing, 85-86, 119
Anointing oil, 46, 47
Antitype, *See* chapter 5
Ark, 31; at Solomon's temple, 33; captured, 32; construction of, 66; contents, 68, 178; David moves it, 33; end of, 33-34; movement of, 32-33; touched brought death, 33; two arks, 178
Ashes, 171
Ash pans, 54
Atonement, 182-87

Bars, 62, 63
Basins, 54
Bedouins, 46
Bells, 82, 83
Bezaleel, 42, 48, 69
Blood, 125, 126; type, 110
Boards, 59
Bonnet, 84
Bowls, 65
Brass, 44, *See* copper
Breastplate, 48, 49, 81, 83, 98
Breeches, 84
Broidered coat, 81, 84, 98
Burnt offering, *See* offerings

Calamus, 47
Candlestick, 62, 162

Cassia, 47
Caul, 125, 127
Censers, 55, 66, 168
Chapters, 44, 51
Cherubim, 58, 61, 67, 183
Christ, 20, 23, 74, 120, 123, 125, 127, 128, 130, 132, 133, 137, 138, 140, 143, 144, 145, 153, 158, 159, 181, 182, 183, 186, 187, 188, 189; *See* chapter 7
Cinnamon, 47
Clothing, 80, 81
Cloud, pillar of, 29
Compass, 54
Confession, 152
Copper, 44, 53
Court of the tabernacle, 50, 51, 52
Covenant, 20; New, 76, 77; Old, 77, 127, 128, 130; *See* New Testament
Coverings, furniture, 96; tabernacle, 45, 56-58
Covers, 66
Cubit, 51
Curtain, goat hair, 45, 58; linen, 45, 51

Day of Atonement, ritual of, 177-89, 182-89; type, 11, 168
Dishes, 65
Door of the tabernacle, 51, 59
Drink offering, *See* offerings
Dugongs, 45

Eleazar, 90, 92
Ephod, 48, 81, 82, 83, 98
Exodus, number of people in, 28
Extremism, 99

Fabrics, 45
Fat, 123, 125, 153

193

Fillets, 44, 51
Firepans, 55, *See* censers
Firstborn, 76, 78, 88, 153
Firstfruit, 145, 153
Flax, 45
Fleshhooks, 54
Frankincense, 47, 65, 143, 144
Freewill offering, *See* offerings
Furniture, type 106, 107

Galbanum, 47
Gate, *See* door of the tabernacle
Gershonites, duties, 88, 91
Gibeonites, 89, 92
Gibeon, 31
Gilgal, 30
Gospel, 23, 74, 102, 104, 162, 180, 181
Grate, 54

Heave offering, *See* offerings
High priest, *See* priest
Holy of holies, 49, 56, 71, 168, 177, 179; type, 107
Holy place, 49, 56, 62, 64, 161; type, 107
Holy Spirit, 164
Honey, 143
Hooks, 44, 51, 59
Horeb *See*. Mount Sinai
Horns, 53, 66, 187

Idolatry, 75
Incense, strange, 48, 169; sweet, 47, 48, 65, 167
Incense altar, *See* altar
Israel, 21, 25
Ithamar, 91, 93

Jesus, *See* Christ
Joshua, 21
Jubilee, 189
Judaism, 20
Justice, 181, 188

Kadesh-barnea, 29
Kidneys, 125-26

Kohathites, duties, 89, 90, 93, 178
Korah, 78, 168

Lamps, 62
Laver, 44, 55-56, 158-59
Law, 21-22, 179, 181-82
Leaven, 143, 146, 166
Levites, 21, 78, 90, 92, 103; *See* chapter 4
Levitical priesthood, 74, 75, 76, 159
Light, 162-63
Linen, 45, 58, 59
Linen curtain, 51

Manna, 68, 166, 167, 178, 179
Meat offering, *See* offerings
Merarites, duties, 89, 91, 93
Mercy, 180, 181
Mercy seat, 66-68, 177, 186
Metals, 43, 44
Mitre, 81, 82-83, 98
Moses, 27, 28, 42, 43, 76-77, 78, 80
Mount Sinai, 21, 27, 28, 29, 30, 41
Myrrh, 47

Nadab, 168
Needlework, 52, 59
New covenant, *See* covenant
New Testament, 100, 101, 104, 115, 116, 120, 126, 127, 134, 158, 163, 188
Nob, 30, 165

Offerings, animals offered, 123-27; animal parts offered, 125; burnt, 121, 122, 139-41, 145; compulsory offerings chart, 155-57; condition of animals, 125; drink, 122, 144, 154; five principal, 122, 27; freewill, 149; heave, 120, 147, 153; heave shoulder, 147; meat, 121, 122, 142-46, 154, 166; most holy and holy, 147; number of yearly, 123; peace, 86, 121, 122, 146-50; ritual of, 150-53; ritual of daily, 170-75; significance of, 127-31; sin, 123-25; sweet- non-sweet, 122; thanksgiving, 86, 149; three kinds of, 148, 153; trespass, 121, 124, 137-39; type, 109, 110; voluntary, 149; vow, 148; wave, 86, 88, 148; wave breast, 147

Index

Oil, olive, 46, 143, 144, 162, 166
Old covenant, *See* covenant
Old Testament, 19, 20, 50, 73, 100, 101, 102, 104, 106, 109, 127, 128, 130, 134, 145, 158, 159, 163, 164, 188, 189
Onyche, 47
Onyx, 48, 81
Opercula, 47
Outer court, *See* court of the tabernacle

Peace offering, *See* offerings
Pentateuch, 20, 179
Pillars, 51, 59, 61
Pins, 51
Plate, gold, 81, 98
Pomegranate, 82, 83, 98
Porpoise, 46
Priest, 106, 109, 110, 111, 119, 133, 135, 138, 153, 155, 158, 159, 168, 170, 172; killed, 30; two high priests, 31, 177-89; type, 105-06, 109-10; *See* chapter 4

Ram skin, 45, 59
Resurrection, 187
Robe, 81, 82, 84

Sacrifices, 54, 120, 121, 123, 129, 130; *See* offerings
Salt, 143-44
Salvation, 20, 22, 23
Sanctuary, 50, 177; *See* tabernacle proper
Scapegoat, 86
Sheep, broadtailed, 125
Shekels, 43
Shewbread, 64-65, 165-67
Shiloh, 21, 30, 74
Shittim wood, 46, 51, 53, 59, 64, 66, 67, 68
Shoe leather, 46
Shoulderpieces, 81, 82
Shovels, 54
Silver, 43, 44
Sin offering, *See* offerings
Skins, badger, 46, 57; ram, 45, 57
Snuffdishes, 54, 63

Sockets, 44, 51, 59, 61
Spices, 46, 47
Spoons, 46, 47
Stacte, 47
Staves, 56, 63, 64, 66, 68
Stones, 48, 49, 81, 98
Strange fire, 168

Tabernacle, another tabernacle, 28; areas of, 49-50; at Gibeon, 30; at Gilgal, 28; at Nob, 30; at Shiloh, 30; at Shittim, 28; burned, 30; construction of, 42; construction time, 28; cost, 50; door of, 51-52; how long used, 32; location, 21; material for construction, 28, 41-42; origin, 25; peaked roof, 58, 63; tabernacle proper, 49, 50; two tabernacles, 30, 33.; type of gospel, 22-23, 102; typology, *See* chapter 5
Table of shrewbread, 64, 65, 165-67
Taches, 58
Talent, 43, 44
Tenons, 59
Thanksgiving offering, *See* offerings
Thummim, 48, 89, 186
Tithes, 94, 153
Trespass offering, *See* offerings
Tribes, 94, 95
Trumpets, 93, 88, 189

Urim, 48, 89, 186
Uzzah, 91
Uzziah, 168

Veil, 52, 59, 61; type, 111, 112, 188
Voluntary offering, *See* offerings
Vow offering, *See* offerings

Walls, 59
Washing, 80, 159
Water of purification, 87
Water of separation, 87
Wave offering, *See* offerings
Wine, 133, 144, 154-56
Wood, 46, *See* shittim wood